TWAYNE'S WORLD AUTHORS SERIES

A Survey of the World's Literature

Sylvia E. Bowman, Indiana University

GENERAL EDITOR

FRANCE

Maxwell A. Smith, Guerry Professor of French, Emeritus
The University of Chattanooga
Former Visiting Professor in Modern Languages
The Florida State University

EDITOR

Alexandre Dumas *père*

TWAS 388

Alexandre Dumas *père* in 1829

ALEXANDRE DUMAS
père

By RICHARD S. STOWE

Lawrence University

TWAYNE PUBLISHERS

A DIVISION OF G. K. HALL & CO., BOSTON

Library of Congress Cataloging in Publication Data

Stowe, Richard S
    Alexandre Dumas (père).

    (Twayne's world authors series; TWAS 388:
France)
    Bibliography: p. 157–60.
    Includes index.
    1. Dumas, Alexandre, 1802–1870.   I. Title.
PQ2230.S84   843'.7   75-43919
ISBN 0-8057-6230-2

FOR NANCY

Contents

About the Author

Richard S. Stowe took his B.A. and Ph.D. degrees at the University of Wisconsin, and his M.A. at the University of California at Los Angeles. His special interest in French theater and fiction of the Romantic period is reflected in his doctoral dissertation on Alfred de Musset and the present study. After teaching French and Spanish for four years at Park College, Parkville, Mo., he joined the faculty of Lawrence University in 1957. He is at present Associate Professor of French language and literature there.

Preface

Few men have crammed as much adventure, activity, passion, and sheer zest for living into sixty-eight years as did the man we call Alexandre Dumas *père*. As a writer, too, he left few domains unexplored. Leaping to fame first through his dramas, Dumas achieved his greatest and most lasting popularity as a novelist, but throughout his life he wrote almost as prolifically in other genres. A true son of the Romantic era, he found in poetry his first form of literary expression. Travel books, volume after volume of memoirs, commentary on historical and contemporary subjects of all sorts poured from his pen, along with a substantial number of short stories, essays, and occasional pieces, all squeezed between his several journalistic ventures and the vast bulk of his better-known works.

Everything about the man seems to be on a giant scale; any study of Dumas *père* or his works, therefore, must necessarily be selective. The number of books, essays, and articles about him is enormous. The standard edition of his *Oeuvres complètes* runs to 301 volumes, but despite its title is not really complete: a few possibly spurious works are included in it, but a greater number of authentic ones are omitted. It must indeed be true, as André Maurois wryly observed in his biography of Dumas, that "no one has read *all* of Dumas; that would be as impossible as for him to have written it all."

The purpose of this brief study is to survey the range of Dumas's literary activity, to give a sense of its scope and variety, and to examine in such detail as space and interest permit those works which critics and time have found most worthy and durable. Many must remain unmentioned or merely touched upon, as will be the case also with a number of scholarly problems and episodes in Dumas's life that bear directly on his work but that are adequately dealt with elsewhere. Our goal is a fair and reasonably comprehensive appraisal of Dumas *père*'s contribution to world literature, a better knowledge of the nature and qualities of his best writing, and some understanding of the special magic that infuses it still for so many readers.

Many persons have helped and encouraged me in many ways during the writing of this book; to all of them I am grateful. Special thanks, however, go to two of my colleagues at Lawrence University, Professors Elizabeth T. Forter and Anne P. Jones; to Virginia J. Hill, Edward Hugdahl, and Dan Church; to Ruth Lesselyong and Dorothy Martinek who prepared the typescript; and to Professor Maxwell Smith, whose patience and understanding were helpful at more than one difficult moment. With one exception (duly noted), all translations are my own; those from Dumas, unless otherwise indicated, are based on the texts of the Lévy edition. Mine too is the responsibility for any errors.

RICHARD S. STOWE

Lourmarin

Chronology

1802 July 24: Birth of Alexandre Dumas in Villers-Cotterêts; name officially amended in 1813 to add "Davy de la Pailleterie."

1806 February 26: Death of Dumas's father.

1818 Dumas meets Adolphe de Leuven and Amédée de la Ponce.

1820– With De Leuven Dumas writes *Le Major de Strasbourg, Le*
1821 *Dîner d'amis*, and *Les Abencérages*.

1822 November: Dumas's first visit to Paris.

1823 Settles in Paris. Enters secretariat of Duc d'Orléans. Chance meeting with Charles Nodier.

1824 July 27: Birth of Alexandre Dumas *fils* to Dumas and Marie-Catherine-Laure Labay, a seamstress. (Mother's surname is frequently given as Lebay.)
       First work by Dumas known to be published: thirty-eight-line poem, "La Rose rouge et la Rose blanche," in *Almanach dédié aux Demoiselles*.

1825 September 22: *La Chasse et l'Amour* at Théâtre de l'Ambigu.

1826 Publishes *Nouvelles Contemporaines* and numerous poems. November 21: First performance of *La Noce et l'Enterrement* at Théâtre de la Porte-Saint-Martin.

1827 Start of three-year liaison with Mélanie Waldor. September 6: First Paris performance by touring English troupe, active there until July, 1828.

1828 Summer: Dumas writes *Henri III et sa cour* in two months.

1829 February 10: First performance of *Henri III* at Comédie-Française; repeated thirty-seven times.
       June: Attends reading of *Un Duel sous Richelieu (Marion Delorme)*.

1830 March 30: Première at Odéon of *Christine*.
       June: Dumas begins liaison with actress Bell Krelsamer (name sometimes given as Krebsamer).
       June-July: Writes *Antony* in six weeks.

1831   January 10: Première, at Odéon, of *Napoléon Bonaparte*. Dumas's first publications in *Revue des Deux-Mondes:* an article, *La Vendée après le 29 juillet;* a story entitled *La Rose rouge; Un Récit de la Terreur;* and two *"scènes historiques."*
        March 5: Birth of Marie-Alexandrine, daughter of Dumas and Bell Krelsamer.
        May 3: Première of *Antony* at Porte-Saint-Martin.
        October 20: *Charles VII chez ses grands vassaux* at Odéon.
        December 10: *Richard Darlington* at Porte-Saint-Martin.
1832   February 6: *Teresa* at Salle Ventadour (Opéra-Comique).
        April 6: *Le Mari de la veuve* at Comédie-Française.
        May 29: Première of *La Tour de Nesle* at Porte-Saint-Martin.
        July-October: Travels in Switzerland; visits Chateaubriand in Lucerne in September.
1833   Dumas's first "historical compilation": *Gaule et France.* First *"impressions de voyage"* *(En Suisse)* appear in *Revue des Deux-Mondes.*
        December 28: *Angèle* at Porte-Saint-Martin.
1834   April 28: Projected revival of *Antony* forbidden by censor.
        June 2: *Catherine Howard* at Porte-Saint-Martin.
        October-November: Tours Provence with painter Godefroy Jadin.
1835   Spends most of year living and travelling in Italy.
1836   *Isabel de Bavière*, first of Dumas's *Chroniques de France.*
        March-April: *Guelfes et Gibelins* and *Gabriel Payot*, Dumas's last contributions to *Revue des Deux-Mondes.*
        August 31: *Kean, ou Désordre et Génie* at Variétés.
1837   July 2: Dumas named Chevalier de la Légion d'Honneur. With Victor Hugo, Dumas secures *privilège* for creation of Théâtre de la Renaissance; new theater opens with *Ruy Blas*.
        October 31: Première at Opéra-Comique of *Piquillo*, music by Hippolyte Monpou, text by Dumas and Gérard de Nerval.
1838   Dumas's real beginning as a novelist: Publishes *La Salle d'armes* (containing two short novels, *Pauline* and *Pascal Bruno); La Comtesse de Salisbury*, his first historical *feuilleton* (serial novel) in *La Presse;* and *Le Capitaine Paul*, a *feuilleton* in *Le Siècle*, reprinted in book form the same year.
        August 1: Death of Dumas's mother, in Paris.

August 19: Dumas goes with Ida Ferrier to Brussels, thence to Frankfurt, where they join Gérard de Nerval; the two men write *Léo Burckart* and *L'Alchimiste* together while travelling in Germany.

October 12: Première, at Théâtre du Panthéon, of *Paul Jones*, five-act drama drawn by Dumas from *Le Capitaine Paul*.

November 30: Nerval introduces Dumas to Auguste Maquet.

1839   January 14: Production of *Bathilde*, Dumas's revision of a play by Maquet—their first collaboration.

April 2: Première of *Mademoiselle de Belle-Isle* at Comédie-Française.

April 10: *L'Alchimiste* at Théâtre de la Renaissance.

April 16: *Léo Burckart* at Porte-Saint-Martin.

1840   February 5: Marriage of Dumas and Ida Ferrier in the church of Saint-Roch, Paris. From June, 1840, until September, 1842, Dumas and his wife live in Florence with occasional brief visits to Paris.

1841   *Nouvelles Impressions de Voyage: Midi de la France; Excursions sur les bords du Rhin.*

June 1: *Un Mariage sous Louis XV* at Comédie-Française.

1842   June: In company with Prince Napoleon, Dumas visits the island of Monte-Cristo.

Serial publication of *Le Chevalier d'Harmental*, first novel based on a preliminary version by Maquet.

1843   July 25: *Les Demoiselles de Saint-Cyr* at Comédie-Française.

Many publications, including *Georges* and *Ascanio*.

1844   *Les Trois Mousquetaires* in *Le Siècle*; immediately reissued in eight volumes.

Le Comte de Monte-Cristo begins in *Journal des Débats*.

July: Dumas purchases land at Port-Marly, where he will build his "Château de Monte-Cristo."

October 15: Friendly separation of Dumas and Ida Ferrier.

1845   *Comte de Monte-Cristo* continues in *Journal des Débats*. *La Reine Margot* in *La Presse; Vingt Ans après* in *Le Siècle*.

February: Eugène de Mirecourt publishes *Fabrique de romans: Maison Alexandre Dumas et Cie*.

May 16: Dumas wins suit for slander against Mirecourt.

October 27: *Les Mousquetaires* at Théâtre de l'Ambigu

(dramatization by Dumas and Maquet of parts of *Vingt Ans après*).

1846   January: Serial and first book publication (eighteen volumes) of *Monte-Cristo* completed.
Le Chevalier de Maison-Rouge in *La Démocratie pacifique;* *La Dame de Monsoreau* in *Le Constitutionnel;* first installments of *Joseph Balsamo* in *La Presse.*
Le Bâtard de Mauléon; Les Deux Diane.
October 3 (until January 15, 1847): Dumas *père* and *fils* tour Spain and Algeria, accompanied by Maquet and Louis Boulanger.

1847   January 22–February 19: Lawsuit brought against Dumas by *La Presse* and *Le Constitutionnel* for failure to supply *feuilletons* he was contracted to provide; judgment adverse to Dumas.
February 20: *La Reine Margot* opens Dumas's Théâtre Historique.
July 27: "Housewarming" party (500–600 guests) at newly completed Château de Monte-Cristo.

1848   February: Ida Ferrier obtains legal separation from Dumas.
March 1: Dumas begins publishing magazine *Le Mois.*
May 20–June 24: Edits and publishes literary daily *La France Nouvelle* (thirty issues only).
Serial publication of *Vicomte de Bragelonne* and *Le Véloce* begins.
Les Quarante-Cinq and *De Paris à Cadix* in book form.

1849   *Le Collier de la Reine* runs in *Le Constitutionnel.*

1850   February 1: Last issue of *Le Mois.*
Vicomte de Bragelonne completed; *La Tulipe noire.*
October: Théâtre Historique closes; Dumas declared bankrupt.

1851   December 7: Goes to Brussels in self-imposed exile.
December 16: Begins publication of *Mes Mémoires* in *La Presse.*

1852   *Olympe de Clèves; Conscience l'Innocent.*

1853   *Ange Pitou;* begins *La Comtesse de Charny* and *Isaac Laquedem.*
October 26: Final installment of *Mes Mémoires* in *La Presse.*
Early November: Settles with creditors, returns to Paris.

November 12: First issue of *Le Mousquetaire*, published daily except Sundays.

1854– *Catherine Blum;* serial publication in *Le Mousquetaire* of *Les*
1855 *Mohicans de Paris* and new series of memoirs, *Souvenirs de 1830 à 1842.*

1857 February: Maquet sues Dumas for payments in arrears and for restitution of rights on certain literary properties.

February 7: Last issue of *Le Mousquetaire.*

April 23: First issue of *Le Monte-Cristo*, "weekly magazine of novels, history, travel and poetry, edited and published by Alexandre Dumas alone."

Le Meneur de loups; Les Compagnons de Jéhu in *Le Journal pour Tous.*

1858 January: Judgment on Maquet's lawsuit gives him 25 per cent of author's rights.

June 15: Dumas leaves on journey to Russia, which lasts until March of following year. *Impressions* written during travels appear regularly in *Le Monte-Cristo.*

1859 March 11: Death of Ida Ferrier Dumas, in Genoa.

1860 February 4: Première at Opéra-Comique of *Le Roman d'Elvire*, by Dumas and de Leuven, music by Ambroise Thomas.

May 10: Last issue of *Le Monte-Cristo.* In same month Dumas leaves for Italy on schooner *Emma* (with Émilie Cordier disguised as cabin boy). Joins Garibaldi in June, enters Palermo and Naples with him in autumn. Founds political journal, *Independente*, in Palermo in November. Publications in France include *Mémoires de Garibaldi* and *Causeries.*

December 24: Birth (in Paris) of Micaëlla-Clélie-Josépha-Élisabeth, daughter of Dumas and Émilie Cordier. Godfather, by proxy, is Garibaldi.

1861– In Italy, Dumas continues to work at prodigious rate. Pub-
1863 lishes *Les Garibaldiens: Révolution de Sicile et de Naples* in 1861. Following year (January-October) he attempts to revive *Le Monte-Cristo.*

1864 April: Dumas returns to Paris.

September 15: Begins publishing *La San-Felice* in *La Presse.*

1866 June and July: Dumas visits Italy, Germany, and Austria. *Les*

Prussiens sur le Rhin (part 1 of *Les Blancs et les Bleus*) in *Les Nouvelles*.

November 18: First issue of new monthly *Le Mousquetaire*.

1867   Parts 2, 3, and 4 of *Les Blancs et les Bleus*.

April 25: Last issue of *Le Mousquetaire*.

1868   Principal publications: *L'Histoire de mes bêtes; Souvenirs dramatiques; Parisiens et provinciaux.*

February 4: Founds *Le Dartagnan* [*sic*]; last issue appears July 4.

July 5: First issue of weekly (Sunday) *Théâtre-Journal*—Dumas's last attempt at journalism.

October 22: Death (aged 74) of Catherine Labay.

1869   March 10: *Les Blancs et les Bleus* performed at Théâtre du Châtelet—Dumas's last play.

March 14: Last issue of *Théâtre-Journal*.

Dumas summers in Brittany, writing *Grand Dictionnaire de cuisine;* unfinished manuscript given to publisher in March, 1870.

1870   In spring goes to South of France for health; returns to Paris on declaration of war (19 July). Suffers stroke and considerable paralysis, is transported to home of son at Puys, on Normandy coast.

December 5: Dumas dies at 10 P.M.

December 8: Temporary interment at Neuville-lès-Pollet.

1872   April 16: Remains transferred to Villers-Cotterêts.

1873   Publication of *Grand Dictionnaire de cuisine*, completed by Anatole France.

1875   Street in Paris named for Dumas.

1883   November 4: Dedication of monument to Dumas by Gustave Doré in Place Malesherbes, Paris.

CHAPTER 1

Preparation for Fame

AT six o'clock in the morning on June 12, 1815, in the little town of Villers-Cotterêts, northeast of Paris, a crowd awaited the arrival of Napoleon, who was on his way to join the troops that, eastward bound, had poured through the village a fortnight earlier. As the emperor's carriage approached the post-house the throng surged forward, a tall, slender thirteen-year-old boy among the first, to see the great man who sat in it brooding, pale, and ill-looking, with his brother Jerome and an aide-de-camp. A brief interchange confirmed where they had stopped and how far they were yet from Soissons; then the emperor withdrew again into his thoughts. A crack of whips, cries of "Vive l'empereur!" and the "gigantic vision" had disappeared.

Echoes of victory, then reports of death drifted back to Villers-Cotterêts in the ensuing days. The 20th of June dawned ominously dark and stormy, and rain fell in torrents. In the afternoon word suddenly spread through the town that ten or twelve so-called Poles had appeared before the town hall, wounded and mud-spattered, bringing tales of a disastrous battle at Waterloo that had annihilated the French army. Unwilling to believe what they heard, the good citizens of Villers-Cotterêts sent the seriously wounded men to the hospital, the others to the town jail. Young Alexandre Dumas, who witnessed this scene as he had the arrival of Napoleon a week before, hurried with his widowed mother to the posting inn where the most reliable news would surely come first.

Only a few hours elapsed before a courier appeared. Half dead with fatigue, he ordered four horses for a carriage that was following on his heels, but refused to say more or to answer any of the eager questions. Scarcely had he set off again before the carriage was heard. The waiting lad asked the innkeeper, "Is it he? Is it the emperor?" "Yes," came the answer as the carriage stopped. It was the emperor, seated as Dumas had last seen him and as forty years later he still remembered him:

It was indeed the same man, indeed the same face—pale, sickly, impassive—but his head was bowed slightly lower on his chest. Was it fatigue? or was it the pain of having gambled for the world and lost?

Like the first time, when he felt the carriage stop he raised his head and peered around with the same vague glance that could become so piercing . . .

"Where are we?" he asked.
"In Villers-Cotterêts, sire."
"Good! Eighteen leagues from Paris?"
"Yes, sire."
"Go on."

And, like the first time, after having asked the same question in nearly the same words, he gave the same order and departed as quickly.[1]

Two days later began a "terrible and magnificent spectacle, sublime in its very hideousness"—the return of the decimated French army, the bedraggled remnants of the proud and confident regiments that had passed through Villers-Cotterêts only weeks before. Following them came the conquerors, Prussians and Englishmen. They too passed on, succeeded by distant rumors of abdication, of exile, and of assassinations, the lingering death throes of the Empire. "Then everything resumed its customary pace and in our little town, far from all disturbances, isolated in its forest, one could almost have believed that nothing had changed. A few people had had a nightmare, that was all."[2]

I *The Air of Two Worlds*

In this episode, so vividly recalled and so revealing of Dumas's keen sense of the dramatic, are reflected two of the most important influences that helped to mold him as man and writer. Born in 1802, Dumas grew up in a France dominated first by the figure, then by the legend of Napoleon. Nurtured on tales of the Ancien Régime and having his own memories of the Empire, he remained always responsive to accounts of valorous deeds, of great acts of patriotism, and of the glory of battle, though he had seen the inglorious consequences of war as well. Without forgetting his father's disillusionment with Napoleon, Dumas's spirit and imagination could still be touched by his brief glimpses of the great man. Romance and adventure were in the air during Dumas's childhood, as truly as they were to be found in the pages of his beloved *Robinson Crusoe* and *Arabian Nights*. These were impressions and enthusiasms he was never to outgrow.

While his imagination was nourished by these heady glimpses of a world outside, the one in which he lived until late adolescence was that of his "little town isolated in its forest"—especially the forest. Its influence on him too was life-long. There he passed an active and happy childhood, roaming fields and woods, hunting, poaching, and running free, all the while developing his powers of observation and absorbing local lore, largely exempt from the constraints of discipline and formal schooling, of which he had little. The clean air of the forest of Villers-Cotterêts was to perfume more than one of the novels of his middle life (as its inhabitants were to people them), and he never had occasion to evoke the landscape of this corner of the Ile-de-France without doing so in most affectionate terms. He revelled in the local fêtes and holidays that added color to country life and tasted the mixed joys of adolescent love, first in a simultaneous "passion" for the niece of his priest and a Spanish friend of hers, later in a deeper, though still passing, attachment to Adèle Dalvin. This liaison was abruptly terminated, when Dumas was nineteen, by the marriage of Adèle to another man. He was not unduly sad to see its end, as by then he was already giving evidence of his capacity for loving sincerely but temporarily and was feeling the tug of ambition and the lure of Paris.

II *Family Background*

Dumas's ancestry reveals a similar juxtaposition of military glory and country life, of grandeur and humbleness. His father, Thomas-Alexandre Dumas Davy de la Pailleterie, was the son of the marquis Antoine-Alexandre Davy de la Pailleterie and a black slave girl, Marie-Cessette Dumas. Born in 1762 in Santo Domingo and brought back to France at the age of eighteen, Thomas-Alexandre eventually enlisted as a private in the army, using Dumas as his name since his father disapproved of the enlistment. Tall, handsome, unbelievably powerful, young Thomas-Alexandre Dumas advanced rapidly in the army after the Revolution, and was apparently as successful in amorous conquests as in military ones. As a lieutenant-colonel, while fighting in the north of France, he met and married Marie-Louise-Élisabeth Labouret, daughter of Claude

Labouret, an innkeeper in Villers-Cotterêts and commanding officer
of the local national guard. The couple was separated almost at once
after the wedding, however, as the wars continued.

Within a year Colonel Dumas was promoted to the rank of general and by age thirty-two he was commander-in-chief of the Army
of the Western Pyrenees. He continued to distinguish himself for
his military prowess and phenomenal strength, but also, his son tells
us in his memoirs, for his humanity and goodness. During Napoleon's Egyptian campaign the general fell into disfavor with
Bonaparte and requested permission to return to France. The return was delayed, however, when the general was imprisoned for
twenty months in Naples—which was then hostile to France—after
a near-disastrous crossing of the Mediterranean. Hardship and
mistreatment during this period left his health permanently
damaged. He finally returned to his wife and eight-year-old daughter in Villers-Cotterêts in May, 1801. On July 24th the following
year his son was born: fair-skinned and blue-eyed, in contrast to his
father, only his hair revealed that he was a quadroon.

General Dumas was especially attached to his son who, in turn,
worshipped him. He spent much of the remaining four years of his
life in unsuccessful attempts to secure financial redress for his
period of imprisonment and to find protectors for little Alexandre
among his former comrades-in-arms who remained in Napoleon's
good graces. When he died his widow and children went to live with
Mme Dumas's parents at their Hôtel de l'Épée. As young Alexandre
grew up Mme Dumas exercised little authority over him, rearing
him with abundant affection but almost in spite of herself letting him
do whatever he wished. Yet the influence of his father stretched
long over Dumas. As he matured the physical and temperamental
resemblances grew apace. He inherited his father's prodigious
strength as well as his fine, small hands and feet. In his exuberance
and imagination, his capacity for enduring loyalty and generosity of
spirit, he also seemed cast in his father's mold.

III   Widening Horizons

Raised thus without the authority of a father, in a loving but poor
home, free and undisciplined, Dumas at seventeen or eighteen was
as learned in the ways of the woods as he was little schooled beyond
reading, writing, and a bit of arithmetic. Independent and alert,
active though hardly industrious by disposition, he was self-reliant,

self-assured to the point of arrogance, and almost totally naive. His imagination fired by the few things he had read—Buffon, the Bible, a taste of classical mythology, the *Arabian Nights*—and by his limited experience of life, he was ripe for the impact of new events and new acquaintances that would arouse his passionate nature and his ambition and lead him beyond his beloved fields and forests. Two men in particular were to offer him the keys to this new world—Amédée de la Ponce and the vicomte Adolphe de Leuven.

De la Ponce, who was an officer in the hussars and the husband of a friend of Dumas's sister, was an intelligent and well-educated man. He took a liking to young Dumas and offered to teach him German and Italian. The language lessons—at least those in German—were less than totally successful, but Dumas credits the hussar with introducing him to Schiller, the Italian writer Ugo Foscolo, and two works that impressed him profoundly: Goethe's *Werther* and G. A. Bürger's ballad *Lenore*. Even more important, as Dumas himself admits, de la Ponce introduced him to the idea of self-discipline and work, an idea scarcely less novel to the carefree youth than the books he explored under his friend's guidance.

It was Adolphe de Leuven, a young Swedish aristocrat,[3] who during summer visits to Villers-Cotterêts first enthralled Dumas with tales of Paris and the theater and who urged him to collaborate on a light comedy, Dumas's first attempt at writing. This one-act piece, *Le Major de Strasbourg*, was in the currently popular patriotic vein, but it was less enthusiastically viewed by producers than by its authors, who proceeded nonetheless to write two more works together—another vaudeville sketch, *Le Dîner d'amis*, and a drama, *Les Abencérages*. De Leuven also brought another influence of decisive importance to bear on Dumas: he introduced him to the works of Sir Walter Scott,[4] thus starting him on the path that would lead to his ultimate triumphs in the realm of historical drama and romance. *Ivanhoe* was the first work of Scott's that Dumas read. Sent to him from Paris by de Leuven, it inspired the first work he wrote alone, a three-act melodrama adapted from it.[5]

Once he was established in Paris, Dumas's passion for the theater and his determination to write increased. He supported himself by working as a copyist in the office of the duc d'Orléans, a post he had secured by virtue of his magnificent, florid handwriting, but he gave every possible moment to reading, writing, and the theater, encouraged and helped by de Leuven's friendship and connections. At the same time he became increasingly aware of the deficiencies in his education. As happened so often in these years, however, a happy coincidence provided the right opportunity at the right time. He relates in his memoirs[6] how the assistant director in his office, Lassagne, not only advised him to read and educate himself, but told him what he most needed to read in preparation for his desired literary career. Lassagne's recommendations included the great French historians and writers of memoirs, from Froissart to Saint-Simon; Homer, Virgil, and Dante; and, among the moderns, Byron, Hugo, Lamartine, and André Chénier. Dumas followed his friend's advice with characteristic enthusiasm and energy, and observed many years later in retrospect: "The horizons that opened before me with each passing moment were so distant that my vision was lost in them."[7]

IV   *The Taste of Success*

Not only his readings, however, but a small theatrical success about this time further encouraged Dumas and intensified his ambition. In 1825 he collaborated with de Leuven and another writer named Rousseau (unrelated to Jean-Jacques) on a comedy with music entitled *La Chasse et l'Amour (Hunting and Love)*, which was produced at the Ambigu on September 22nd of that year and printed soon afterwards. It was a conventional little entertainment, filled with stock characters, predictable situations, and dialogue as obvious as it often was stilted; the songs all used tunes from other currently popular shows. The plot involved a heroine betrothed to an elderly oafish huntsman though she really loved a young man approved of by her mother but not by her father. An embarrassing miscalculation by the hunter, who mistook his fiancée's father for a stag he had been tracking, brought about the inevitable happy ending.

Though it reveals in many ways the youth and inexperience of its authors, *La Chasse et l'Amour* is a not totally unskillful example of its genre. It is trivial, of course, but swift-moving, lively, and sufficiently amusing—whatever its lack of subtlety or sophistication—to make its modest success quite understandable. It interests us today chiefly for the hints it gives already of Dumas's typical verve, good humor, and sense of what would please an audience.

Some fourteen months later another *vaudeville* of Dumas's—this time written jointly with Lassagne and a "play doctor" named Vulpian—reached the stage. A mediocre though mildly entertaining bit of exotica inspired by the tales of Sinbad the Sailor, *La Noce et l'Enterrement (The Wedding and the Burial)* enjoyed forty performances at the Théâtre de la Porte-Saint-Martin, for each of which Dumas received five francs. This time the scene of the action was "on an island adjacent to Malabar" and the characters bore pseudo-oriental names as well as costumes, but the devices were the same: conventional parody, pun-filled dialogue, an array of songs, ensembles, and choruses utilizing already popular melodies. Again, as in the case of *La Chasse et l'Amour*, the playbills did not carry Dumas's name; but if these two early works did not bring him fame—and even Dumas himself seems not to have taken them too seriously—they at least brought him both experience and some much needed money.

Now surer all the time that he had found his way, Dumas opened his eyes and mind to everything, and everything in turn was revelation to him. He gloried in the opportunities to see and be moved by—as well as to meet—the great actors of the day. He was transported by the Shakespearean performances of a company of touring English actors, including Macready, Edmund Kean, Kemble, and Harriet Smithson.[8] And he enjoyed to the full both the friendship of Charles Nodier, whom he had met by chance at a theater soon after his arrival in Paris, and the doors opened for him by that friendship. Nodier enthusiastically endorsed *Christine*, Dumas's first attempt at historical tragedy in verse, when it was presented to the reading committee of the Comédie-Française. Even more important for the budding author, in 1828 Nodier opened to him the doors of his salon at the Arsenal Library.[9] There at the regular Sunday evening receptions he met the leaders of the Romantic movement—Vigny, Lamartine, Hugo and, later, Balzac, Musset, Mérimée, Delacroix—and himself became a part of the group.

Finally, in 1829, with the success of *Henri III et sa cour (Henry the Third and His Court)*, Dumas's fortune and reputation were made. The naive, ignorant provincial who had come to Paris seven years earlier had found both his vocation and his audience.

CHAPTER 2

The Dramatist: Creation and Exploration

I *Historical Drama:* Henri III et sa cour

D UMAS has recounted in his memoirs[1] the story of the writing and the success of *Henri III et sa cour*, and most of his biographers follow his account with only minor modifications or corrections. The idea for the play came to him, Dumas says, by accident or, more accurately, by a singular stroke of good luck when he least expected it. The original version of his tragedy *Christine* had been accepted, subject to some revision, by the Comédie-Française, then indefinitely postponed. One day, stepping into a colleague's office to borrow some paper, Dumas noticed an open book lying on a table. The book was Anquetil's *Esprit de la Ligue*[2]; in it Dumas read an anecdote about one of the *mignons* of King Henri III, Saint-Mégrin, and his love for the wife of his enemy the duc de Guise. His curiosity aroused, Dumas consulted the *Biographie universelle*, which referred him in turn to the memoirs of L'Estoile. There he read not only more about Saint-Mégrin but also the story of Bussy d'Amboise and the Lady of Monsoreau. "It was from this paragraph about Bussy and the one about Saint-Mégrin," he concludes, "that I made my play."

Written in a scant two months, *Henri III* was enthusiastically received at three readings Dumas gave for friends in September, 1828. At the third reading five actors were also present: Firmin (who had arranged the gathering), Michelot, Samson, Mlle Mars, and Mlle Leverd. All of them were eventually to play major roles in the production and it was their urging that made a special reading to the committee of the Théâtre-Français possible. The committee was as enthusiastic as Dumas's friends had been; arrangements were quickly completed, rehearsals and work on the production were begun, and the première was scheduled for February 10, 1829.[3] The weeks before the opening were saddened by the serious illness of Dumas's mother, who was unable to attend the performance, but that was the only flaw in Dumas's triumph when the great night finally arrived. The glory of the occasion for him was completed by the presence—on Dumas's bold personal invitation—of the duc d'Orléans and a party of his friends, who rose to their feet in homage to the author at the end of the performance, while the great soprano Maria Malibran clutched at a pillar to avoid falling as she leaned far out of her box, also overcome by the emotions of the evening.[4]

Despite its faults and weaknesses, which critics began to point out soon enough, the play was not undeserving of its success. It was colorful, vital, new. What it lacked in subtlety it more than made up for in excitement and movement. A historical period was vividly, if superficially, recreated and its heroes were strikingly evoked. Dialogue was crisp and vigorous; though not particularly distinguished, Dumas's prose was swift-moving and serviceable. Once the exposition was over the drama swept on from climax to climax with relentless speed and logic, and with an unerring sense of what would be theatrically effective. Flamboyant and Romantic it was, but it worked. Thus, a year before *Hernani*, Romanticism triumphed in the Théâtre-Français, *foyer* of French Classicism. Its victory that night in 1829 was fairly earned and was no less genuine or important for being a less deliberate attack on tradition than Hugo's drama was to be.

Henri III et sa cour opens in the *cabinet de travail* of Como Ruggieri, an astrologer, on Sunday July 20, 1578. Catherine de Médicis arrives, masked, to inform and instruct Ruggieri with respect to her plans for overcoming Henri, duc de Guise (known as *le balafré*— "Scarface"), and the Ligue. In the duke she sees the greatest threat to her son, King Henri III, and, therefore, to herself and her power. Catherine's plan is to capitalize on her knowledge of the love between Saint-Mégrin, one of the king's *mignons*, and the duchesse de Guise. Knowing that Saint-Mégrin and two of his friends are coming to visit Ruggieri to have their horoscopes cast, Catherine has had the duchess drugged and transported here to be concealed until Saint-Mégrin comes and Ruggieri can arrange a *tête-à-tête*. Everything occurs as planned, but the love scene between Saint-Mégrin and the duchess is interrupted by the arrival of the duc de Guise. The duchess escapes, but leaves a handkerchief. Finding it, her husband realizes that she and Saint-Mégrin—whom the duke has seen and talked with—must have had a rendezvous. The act ends with the duke's dramatic and terrifying cry for vengeance.

The second act takes place in the Louvre the next day. Though rich in details of local color and introducing a number of new characters, it neither drags nor distracts the spectator from the steady development of action set up in Act I. Henri III enters to grant official pardon and to reinstate among his *mignons* the disgraced and exiled courtier Antraguet. Henri de Guise arrives to petition the king for formal recognition of the Ligue and appointment of its leader. His power-seeking is evident and clearly irritates Henri III. Indirectly on behalf of the king, Saint-Mégrin provokes a duel with de Guise; his second will be Bussy d'Amboise, and de Guise asks Antraguet to serve as his. After promising to grant the duc de Guise's requests and announcing that he will watch the duel, Henri III remains alone with his mother, who then reveals fully her artful control over her son. The curtain falls on an atmosphere of quiet menace that contrasts superbly with the violent end of Act I, yet manages to build even greater suspense.

The third act opens in the prayer room of the duchesse de Guise, where the light banter of Arthur, her page, and two ladies-in-waiting introduces an effective contrast of tone at the same time it advances the plot by revealing to the duchess that Arthur is aware of her feelings for Saint-Mégrin and will be her faithful ally. The tone changes abruptly with the arrival of the duke, who dismisses Arthur and brutally tries to force an admission of illicit love. When the duchess persists in affirming her innocence, the duke resorts to physical violence and finally forces her to write a note to Saint-Mégrin inviting him to her room that night and enclosing her key. The curtain is highly dramatic as Arthur is dispatched with the letter and the duchess is locked in her room to await Saint-Mégrin.

The action moves even more precipitately, if possible, in Act IV. Arthur delivers the note to an enraptured Saint-Mégrin in the Louvre. Ruggieri arrives and ominously predicts death for Saint-Mégrin before morning. Upon this, the king and his entourage enter. accompanied by the duc de Guise and his men. To the consternation of the duke and the *ligueurs*, Henri III proclaims himself head of the Ligue. Left alone with the king, Saint-Mégrin suggests that the king has only gained a little time by this move and urges the imprisonment of de Guise. The king delays Saint-Mégrin's departure, but finally the latter sets out for the rendezvous as a violent storm breaks.

Alone in her chamber, the duchess is frantically hoping that Saint-Mégrin will not appear. As one o'clock strikes and she hears the outer doors being closed, she breathes more easily—only to hear Saint-Mégrin's footsteps and the key in the lock. When he enters she tells him of the trap and begs him to flee. He believes only that she does not love him. Again she declares her love and pleads for his escape. A rope with a note from Arthur is thrown in through the window just before the duke starts pounding and shouting at the door. Saint-Mégrin slips out of the window, into the arms of the duke's waiting men. Arthur is killed by them too, and when the duke's henchman calls that Saint-Mégrin is wounded but still breathing, in a final irony the duke tosses down the duchess's handkerchief so that he may be strangled to death with it.

Hippolyte Parigot has observed that Dumas wrote from native dramatic sense, not according to a system: "Dumas does not start from an idea; he does not consciously build antitheses. . . . It is simply the conflict of personalities and situations that effects the mixture [of genres and emotions]."[5] As for the famous classical unities, in this play Dumas clearly violated only one—the unity of place—and that because it served his needs, not because he wished to challenge the principle. He very nearly observed the limit of twenty-four hours imposed by the convention of time, and the simplicity of a single action was absolutely essential if he was to achieve the speed and dramatic intensity that were among his chief aims. But if Dumas composed without theories to elucidate, he did not do so without constant awareness of the way his drama was put together. He remained justly proud of the structure of *Henri III et sa cour*, and wrote of it thus in his memoirs some twenty-five years later:

It is in connection with *Henri III* that one may most easily see that the dramatic sense [*faculté*] is innate to certain men. I was twenty-five years old; *Henri III* was my second serious work: if a conscientious critic should take it and submit it to the most rigorous study, he would find almost everything to reproach in the style, nothing in the structure. I have written fifty plays since *Henri III*; none is more skillfully made.[6]

This judgment is somewhat exaggerated and simplified, as the facts of history were exaggerated and simplified by Dumas in the play, but it remains valid as far as it goes. There is indeed much to take exception to in matters of style,[7] though the dialogue is never lacking in verve and force; and examination of the text easily reveals its inexorable dramatic logic. Each event leads naturally to the next; all the insights and plans set forth in the first act work themselves out directly and convincingly. The spectator, his interest and sympathies clearly engaged, in no doubt as to which side is good and which is bad, is swept on breathlessly. Details of historical color and characterization enrich the sense of period reality without slowing in the least the headlong rush of action. Melodrama? Of course, but surely first-rate melodrama and surely *savamment fait*, as Dumas put it.

The third act most clearly shows how Dumas combined the "two paragraphs" from L'Estoile to form the heart of his play and to achieve the tight structure on which he prided himself. The anecdote about the duc and duchesse de Guise involved, as does the third act of the play, a brutal attempt by the duke to extort a confession from his wife. In history, however, the duke was apparently unconcerned about his wife's fidelity, and was really play-acting when he confronted her with evidence and forced the terrified woman to choose between a dagger and a cup of poison. Hours after the unfortunate duchess had drained the cup and was still awaiting the death she believed certain, the duke informed her that the "poison" had in fact been only consommé.

Of this anecdote, of course, Dumas retained only the identity of the characters and the cruel violence of their confrontation. That much he fitted into the story of Bussy d'Amboise, which provided him with the false assignation arranged by the husband and its grisly consequences. At the same time, having the duc de Guise as his villain made it possible for Dumas to place this story within the larger context of the power struggle involving the Ligue, Henri III, and Catherine de Médicis. In this way relationships and motivations were clarified—however much historical fact was distorted in the process—and a broad panorama of the time was evoked.[8] The unity and intensity of the central action were heightened rather than compromised, while the scope of the drama was extended to embrace the fate of the nation as well as that of the unhappy lovers.

Such qualities and such achievements as these overrode—and still override—superficial drawing of characters, stilted exposition, and occasionally naive application of local color, and help to explain the play's success. For though simple, the characters were convincing, and the violence rang true to a generation that still remembered the Revolution and the Empire, that had thrived on melodrama in the theater. The rapid action and artfully managed *coups-de-théâtre*, the echoes of Shakespeare, Scott, and Schiller, all satisfied the cravings of an excitement-seeking generation that also felt nostalgia for a glorious national past. In *Henri III et sa cour* Dumas achieved exactly what he had set out to achieve. Fortunately, what he offered was also precisely what his public most wanted that February evening in 1829.

The success of *Henri III et sa cour* and the sale of the manuscript the next day for 6,000 francs brought Dumas both fame and temporary relief from financial worries. Threats of having the play closed by the censors and a growing number of adverse criticisms of Dumas and his play did not seriously or long affect Dumas's feelings of satisfaction and confidence. By the end of the month *La Cour du Roi Pétaud (The Court of King Pétaud)* was playing at the Vaude-ville. Written by Cavé, Ferdinand Langlé, and Adolphe de Leuven with Dumas's blessing (and help), it was a scene by scene parody of *Henri III et sa cour* and sure proof of that play's hold on the Parisian public.

II *Historical Tragedy:* Christine

As the excitement of his new status levelled off, Dumas began thinking again of his verse tragedy *Christine*. A seventy-two-hour trip to Le Havre gave him the change of scene and the solitude necessary to work out in his mind the revisions he wanted to make, principally the division into three episodes—Stockholm, Fontainebleau, and Rome—and the addition of the new character Paula. Upon his return, before he could get this new version down on paper, Dumas was invited by Victor Hugo to a reading of his new historical drama *Un Duel sous Richelieu* (later renamed *Marion Delorme*). Dumas went and, in his own words,[9] was overcome by the magnificence of Hugo's style and awareness of the deficiencies of his own. Yet the reading of *Marion Delorme*—again Dumas himself says it[10]—did more than merely impress him. It inspired him. It "opened totally unknown horizons" in poetic effects and devices for him, and it gave him the first idea for his next play, *Antony.* But before undertaking that contemporary drama Dumas returned to *Christine:*

The day after the reading of *Marion Delorme* I had set to work with unbelievable drive. Before the music of the verse I had heard the night before had melted away I was at work, lulled by its fading harmonies; and the new *Christine* opened her eyes to the distant, melodious echo still alive in my soul though its sound had died.[11]

"The new *Christine*" was soon completed and read to Dumas's friends, but the censors refused permission to produce it. Early in 1830, however, Harel—the managing director of the Odéon theater—secured the play from the Comédie-Française as well as the necessary authorization to stage it. Harel was even able to use the same actors who had just performed in an unsuccessful play on the same subject by Dumas's friend Frédéric Soulié. Dumas's "dramatic trilogy in five acts and in verse, with prologue and epilogue," *Christine, ou Stockholm, Fontainebleau et Rome*, received its first performance just a little more than a month after the tumultuous première of *Hernani*. This performance, like that of Hugo's drama, was the occasion of a battle; and, though general approval and enthusiasm ultimately seemed to overcome the protests of those who disliked the play, there was no repetition of the definitive initial success of *Henri III*.

As he watched the stage and the audience, Dumas became acutely aware—even without all of his opponents' vociferous promptings—of cuts and changes that still needed to be made and of some hundred lines of verse that would unquestionably have to be rewritten before the next evening's performance. But how was all that to be done? Prepared in advance for another unalloyed triumph, Dumas had invited twenty or twenty-five friends to supper at his apartment in the rue de l'Université following the play. Now, he felt, he could not withdraw the invitation, nor could he simply leave them to their own devices. Despite the play's uncertain reception the guests came, and while the others ate, drank, and sang with their host in one room, Victor Hugo and Alfred de Vigny took the manuscript and slipped quietly into another. There the two men worked steadily for four hours, cutting and polishing, rewriting completely the hundred objectionable lines, then left the revised manuscript prominently displayed on the mantelpiece when they slipped out again, past the sleeping Dumas. The performance of *Christine* the second night was, Dumas reports, unequivocally a success.[12]

Though Dumas retains the broad outlines of the events in the life of Queen Christina of Sweden that form the subject of his play, he telescopes the action whenever it suits his purpose (e.g., the burial of Descartes and the abdication of Christina both occur in Act II, though they were separated in actuality by more than four years) and he does not hesitate to introduce a major nonhistorical character—Paula—whose mere presence alters both events and motives considerably. The reduction of plot to three major episodes (not symmetrically disposed among the acts) helps to simplify the action, though the breathtaking speed of *Henri III* is never attained. Alternating with tense, dramatic moments are a number of soliloquies and semilyrical dialogues in which the characters examine their feelings and situations. Though certainly not without interest, these passages seem more appropriate to conventional tragedy and tend to work against the suspense that Dumas tries to build elsewhere in his play.

After characters and relationships are established in the Prologue and Act I, the action proper begins in Act II with Christina's announcement of her abdication. She prepares to depart from Sweden with the ambitious Italian nobleman Monaldeschi in her retinue; Paula, a young woman in love with Monaldeschi but disguised as a boy, accompanies them as Christina's page. Act III takes place five years later, in the palace of Fontainebleau. Monaldeschi reveals to the ever-faithful (and still disguised) Paula that his ambition has involved him in active plotting against Christina, who is now interested in regaining the Swedish throne. A rather effective digression from the central action occurs here when Christina is visited by the playwright Corneille, who recites to her some passages from *Cinna* in which the Emperor Augustus displays clemency toward those who have conspired against him. At this point, of course, Christina is unaware of Monaldeschi's schemes, but soon thereafter she intercepts some letters which reveal his perfidy. She engages Sentinelli, captain of her guards, to perform the "execution" of Monaldeschi, which occurs—after several delays, melodramatic confrontations, and the suicide of Paula—at the end of Act V. The Epilogue, set in Rome and the only episode precisely dated by Dumas (19 April 1689), has Sentinelli, now an old holy man, coming to pray for the dying Christina. When he realizes who she is he reveals his own identity, and together they speak of their lives and regrets since the execution-assassination of Monaldeschi. The play ends with Christina's death.

Not a hopelessly bad play, *Christine* is not really a very good one either. Some highly effective scenes and powerful curtains stand beside lengthy stretches that are awkward or contrived. Dumas sensed the drama in the life of Christina and the death of Monaldeschi, but he has not fully conveyed it. Since his verse is rarely distinguished and sometimes quite bad, *Christine* on the whole gains little if anything from its poetic form except, perhaps, a degree of dignity and appropriate stateliness of movement in a few scenes. The net result is a play that achieves neither the poetic nobility and psychological depth of tragedy nor the frank melodrama of *Henri III et sa cour*, while seeming to strive for both. No small part of the success it did have, as Dumas himself acknowledged in a postscript to the printed text, was surely due to the inspired performances of the actors, especially Mlle George as Christina and Lockroy as Monaldeschi, Alexandrine Noblet as Paula and Ligier as the captain of the queen's guards, Sentinelli. They all believed in the characters they portrayed and performed with a passionate intensity that must have given their roles an apparent depth and reality they only fitfully suggest on the printed page.

III   *Drame moderne:* Antony

Soon after the production of *Christine* Dumas began work on *Antony*, which he completed in six weeks of feverish writing.[13] Accepted by the Théâtre-Français, after several delays the new play was cast and put into rehearsal. The actors were unhappy with their roles, however, causing further delays on various pretexts and plaguing Dumas with requests for changes or cuts until finally, near despair, he withdrew the play. Still anxious to have it produced, Dumas read his manuscript to the popular actress Marie Dorval. She was wildly enthusiastic about the role of Adèle, urged Dumas to undo the cuts and changes he had made, and suggested the actor Bocage for the title role. Dorval and Bocage then aided Dumas in persuading the reluctant manager of the Théâtre de la Porte-Saint-Martin to stage the work, which was at last performed eleven months after Dumas had finished writing it.

Meanwhile, during the negotiations with the Théâtre-Français and the early weeks of rehearsal there, Dumas had written for the producer Harel a historical drama in twenty-four scenes entitled *Napoléon Bonaparte*. Literally imprisoned by Harel,[14] Dumas ground the play out in eight days. It was performed with considerable success (and many cuts) at the Odéon in January, 1831, but it was a source of neither pride nor real satisfaction to Dumas. Intended purely to capitalize on the growing vogue for things Napoleonic, the play fulfilled its purpose well but possessed little intrinsic quality or originality. Dumas attributed its success entirely to its subject matter, its lavish, spectacular production, and the performance of Frédérick Lemaître as Napoleon. Of the play itself, Dumas stated flatly—and with justice: "It was not good . . . its success was purely circumstantial; its literary worth was virtually nil."[15]

Antony, however, was another matter. Dumas was deeply involved emotionally in the play, drawn as it was to a great extent from his own life and experience, and he believed strongly in its worth as a play both for its characters and dramatic intensity and because, like *Henri III*, it represented a new theatrical genre—in this case the *drame moderne.*

"*Antony* is not a drama," Dumas wrote later in his memoirs, "*Antony* is not a tragedy, *Antony* is not a play. *Antony* is an episode of love, of jealousy, of anger, in five acts. Except for the murder, I was Antony; except for the flight, she was Adèle."[16] "She" was Mélanie Waldor, with whom Dumas had had a liaison, begun in 1827 but now over, at least as far as he was concerned. The impassioned and increasingly theatrical letters he wrote to her during their love affair are echoed, indeed frequently almost quoted, in the dialogue of *Antony*. In the wake of Dumas's candid acknowledgments, his biographers have traced in detail the many other reflections of the liaison in the play's action and situations. But of considerably greater importance to the development of the theater in nineteenth century France was Dumas's decision to place his drama in a concretely contemporary setting and, to a markedly greater degree than in *Henri III et sa cour*, to make the drama and its historical context inseparably interdependent. The action was to grow not only from the characters and their relationships but from the conflicts between their needs or desires and the social institutions and mores of the day. Though it remains true that Dumas had no dramatic system, that he wrote without formal theories, here again we can see that there was full awareness of what he was doing. However much his dramatic sense may have been instinctive, it was never unconscious.

In structure *Antony* anticipates the *pièce bien faite*—the well-

made play—which was to dominate Parisian stages for decades. It is,
if anything, more skillfully constructed than *Henri III*, of which
Dumas remained so proud; its greatest strengths are its fundamental
simplicity, the careful preparation of every event, and the absence
of anything extraneous.

The action can be briefly summarized. The mysterious Antony,
whose secret—his illegitimate birth—will be revealed in Act II,
returns to Paris after a three year absence and seeks an interview
with Adèle d'Hervey, the young matron whom he had loved and
apparently abandoned on his departure. Having married and had a
daughter in the interim, Adèle is understandably reluctant to see
Antony again and risk reviving the ill-suppressed passion she still
feels for him. Leaving her house in order to be gone when he
arrives, Adèle is saved from a carriage accident by Antony, who
halts her runaway horses but is seriously hurt himself. He is carried
into Adèle's house, where the doctor orders him to stay until he
recovers fully.

Concerned for her reputation and unsure of her ability to resist
Antony and her undimmed love for him, Adèle decides to run away
and join her husband, Colonel d'Hervey, who is stationed in
Strasbourg. Infuriated by the letter she leaves for him, Antony
rushes ahead of Adèle and prepares a trap for her in an inn, the last
relay stop before Strasbourg. Once there, Adèle finds herself unable
to pursue her journey to Strasbourg, is confronted by Antony, and,
in mingled terror and love, is subjugated by him.

Three months later Adèle re-enters Parisian social life at a soirée
given by her friend the vicomtesse de Lacy. Antony is also invited
and, when Adèle is maliciously taxed with immorality by one of the
ladies present, Antony defends her virtue and denounces society for
false values and hypocrisy. Adèle, distressed, hurries home,
followed directly by Antony, who has just been warned that Colonel
d'Hervey is en route home from Strasbourg and will arrive soon.
Unwilling to run off with Antony and abandon her husband and
daughter for fear of what her consequent disgrace would do to them,
Adèle can only plead for death. As the colonel arrives and pounds on
the door, Antony embraces Adèle, then stabs her. When the door
breaks down and Colonel d'Hervey leaps into the room, Antony, in
a final attempt to protect Adèle, utters the famous curtain line: "She
resisted me so I killed her!"

On this framework of straightforward and violent action Dumas has hung social commentary, ideas about the contemporary theater—specifically, his concept of the *drame moderne*—and introduced at least one theme which was to preoccupy French playwrights for a hundred years or more, the adulteress. He has also, in Antony himself, created one of the most perfect examples of the doomed Romantic hero, the man at once superior to and rejected by society, who in turn rejects society and denies its rights over him.

The social issues which dominate the play, contemporary then and not yet completely resolved in our own day, are the problems associated with illegitimacy and the status of women. They are not introduced gratuitously or incidentally, however. Part of the fabric of character and situation, they are integral to the drama. Antony could not marry Adèle when she was free because, though he could offer her wealth, he could not offer her a name. "You seemed to me," says Adèle to Antony in Act II, scene 4, "born for all ranks, called to fill all stations in life . . . able to do anything."

"Alas, Madame," he replies, "before my birth, before I could do anything about it, fate destroyed all such possibilities; and from the day I first became aware of myself, everything that for anyone else would have been positive and real, for me was only dream and deception." In the following scene, again speaking to Adèle, Antony denounces not fate so much as the society that perpetuates these prejudices:

These two words, shame and misfortune, attached themselves to me like two evil spirits . . . . I tried to overcome prejudice by educa- tion . . . . Arts, languages, science. I studied everything, learned every- thing . . . . What a fool I was to enlarge my heart so that despair could lodge in it! Natural gifts or acquired knowledge, everything dis- appeared in the face of the stain of my birth: careers open to the most mediocre of men were closed to me; I had to give my name, and I had no name. Oh, why wasn't I born poor and left ignorant! Lost among the lower classes, at least there I wouldn't have been pursued by prejudice . . . .

The controversy which erupted in the press over such speeches—arguments as to whether or not the prejudice existed and whether or not Dumas's charges were justified—was in itself ample evidence that the issue was a live one still.[17] And, though earlier writers—most notably Beaumarchais and Diderot—were cited as having already dealt with the question, Dumas's approach was

clearly new. Underscoring the conflict between individual and
society, he treated the problem neither philosophically nor morally
so much as in concrete social and psychological terms. Antony's
character, his attitudes, and his social status are all directly traceable
to the accident of his birth.

Correspondingly, the conflicts faced by Antony and Adèle are
intensified by her inability to reject the values and obligations that
society imposes on her as a woman. From start to finish of the play,
Adèle is torn between her passion for Antony and her obsession with
her reputation and its effect, in society's eyes, on the husband she
respects and the daughter she loves. "The world has its laws," she
says to Antony [Act II, scene 5], "and society has its
demands . . . . Even if I did not want to, I would have to accept
them." Antony may revolt, then, but Adèle cannot—indeed, will
not. At the end she chooses death as the only escape from her
dilemma, the only possible means of saving a shred of her honor. In
making this choice she falls victim to society and raises the question
of why it should be so. Implicitly, then, but no less certainly her fate
brings into question contemporary ideas on marriage, adultery, and
the status of women in society as it was then constituted. As in the
case of Antony's illegitimacy, Dumas again approaches the issues in
terms of their social implications rather than as moral or religious
questions.

Yet, because Dumas makes these social concerns so intrinsic a
part of the characters and action of the drama, *Antony* remains the
"episode of passion" that he intended it to be. In no sense does it
ever become a social tract, a *pièce à thèse*. The same may be said
with respect to the literary ideas introduced in the fourth act.
Though many critics have seen there both statement and defense of
Dumas's ideas about the *drame moderne* that he was, in fact,
creating with this play,[18] in the literary discussion at the vicomtesse
de Lacy's soirée Dumas never oversteps the limits of the dramatic
context. The search for literary inspiration in contemporary life is an
appropriate subject for discussion in its place here, and it is carefully
linked to events, both past and present, in the story of Adèle and
Antony. Indeed, this literary conversation specifically provides
occasion for the public embarrassment of Adèle and for Antony's
vigorous defense of her virtue and attack on society's values. At the
same time, the ideas advanced in this episode unquestionably
illuminate Dumas's feelings about the *drame moderne*, and their

interest is not lessened for their being thus incorporated into the dialogue and action.

Dumas first acknowledges and justifies the public's desire to see contemporary persons and events on the stage, thus implicitly justifying also his own decision to set his play in modern times. Then, through his playwright character Eugène d'Hervilly, Dumas points out the difficulty of what he is trying to do. By making all men equal, his spokesman observes, the Revolution has made the contemporary comedy of manners a genre almost impossible to write in and has left only the *drame,* whose province is the depiction of passions. When the resemblance between the actor's passions and those of the spectator becomes too close, the spectator may claim to find the drama false, exaggerated, and melodramatic for lack of the perspective which historical drama would give him. But the dramatist is not, for this, to be relieved of his obligation to provide the public with what it asks for and to depict contemporary passions faithfully.[19]

Simply as a play, apart from any social and literary issues involved or embodied in it, *Antony* is characteristic of Dumas at his flamboyant and melodramatic best. Like *Henri III et sa cour* it spoke directly to its audience in the language that audience wanted to hear. While reflecting changes in public taste in its subject and setting, *Antony* retained many of the earlier play's most striking and perennially appealing features. The public found in it the same pace and suspense (Dumas even ordered short intermissions so no momentum would be lost between acts); the same vividly defined characters and sharply observed—though less obviously applied— details of local color; the same liberal use of violence. The spectacular curtains were still there too—for example, Antony ripping the bandages off his wounds at the end of Act I, and wordlessly leading Adèle to the bedroom in the inn at the end of Act III—as was the faultlessly maintained, steadily rising crescendo of action from the opening scene until the final, harrowing *coup de théâtre.*

Small wonder, then, that *Antony* was an even greater popular success than *Henri III et sa cour,* despite a far from uniform or complimentary reaction on the part of the critics; or that, as Maurois points out, it actually created a greater sensation than the opening of *Hernani.*[20] In a lifetime of theatrical successes Dumas probably knew no greater triumph than this. And, though it did not remain

long on the boards—banned by the censors in 1834, it was not
revived in France until 1867, is virtually never performed, and is
only rarely read in more recent years—*Antony* cast a long shadow.
One can with justice summarize its importance in the words of
Albert Thibaudet, who wrote in his *Histoire de la littérature
française de 1789 à nos jours:*

In effect *Antony* created that simple and supple dramatic reality that is
called the play, the modern play in prose, which twenty years later, with
the next generation, would become the common definitive language of the
theater.[21]

IV *Melodrama Triumphant:* La Tour de Nesle

Almost all of Dumas's plays were successful when they were
produced, but no Romantic drama—by him or anyone else—
enjoyed so sustained a public triumph as *La Tour de Nesle (The
Tower of Nesle)*, which received almost eight hundred consecutive
performances[22] after its première at the Théâtre de la Porte-Saint-
Martin on May 29, 1832. While lacking the historical importance of
Henri III et sa cour and *Antony, La Tour de Nesle* remains today
probably the best known of Dumas's plays, the very model of
"historical" melodrama; surprisingly, it was first performed and
published as the work of Frédéric Gaillardet.

Gaillardet, a young man from the provinces, had brought to the
producer Harel a play he had written based on popular—and
gruesome—legends attached to the person of Marguerite de
Bourgogne, wife of Louis X of France. Though quite untrue, the
tales had been recounted with relish by Brantôme in the sixteenth
century and already alluded to by Villon in his *Ballade des Dames
du temps jadis* a century earlier: ". . . où est la roine/Qui commanda
que Buridan/Fust jeté en un sac en Seine?" Harel liked the play and
wanted to produce it, but found it unperformable as Gaillardet had
written it. At Harel's request, the critic Jules Janin rewrote it,
improving the style and adding one or two long speeches, but Harel
found the play no more actable and so approached Dumas. The
latter's imagination was caught by the subject and his theatrical
sense perceived at once the necessary changes: an additional scene
at the beginning to establish the characters and situation, other
added scenes (most notably the prison scene in Act III) and
dialogue, revised curtains, and a new conception of the play as "the

struggle between Buridan and Marguerite de Bourgogne, between an adventurer and a queen, the one armed with all the resources of his genius, the other all the power of her rank."[23] (Naturally, Dumas continues in his memoirs, genius would triumph over power.) In his hands the play was quickly and almost completely rewritten then, with virtually nothing remaining of Gaillardet's efforts except the core of plot, and of Janin's only the famous *tirade* delivered by Buridan on the subject of *"les grandes dames."*

Harel readily accepted Dumas's request for 10 per cent of the gross receipts (leaving intact the remuneration originally promised to Gaillardet), but only after a struggle did he yield to Dumas's insistence that his name not appear as author. The first posters and playbills announced the play as by "MM. Frédéric Gaillardet and ***"; the day after the opening Harel changed them to read "By MM. *** and F. Gaillardet," thus unleashing a series of bitter exchanges by letter and in the press, an equally acrimonious lawsuit, and eventually (in 1834) an inconclusive duel between Dumas and Gaillardet. At the same time, of course, Harel succeeded in his real aim of making sure that all Paris knew of Dumas's contribution to the play, but it was not until twenty-nine years later that Gaillardet—having been legally declared sole author in 1832—relented and allowed Dumas's name to appear on playbills as co-author with him. The published play did not bear Dumas's name until his *Théâtre complet* was issued by Michel Lévy shortly thereafter.

At the beginning of the thirteenth century there stood, across the Seine from the Louvre, the Tower of Nesle, protecting city and river within the enclosing walls built by Philippe-Auguste. Tall and mysterious, with few and narrow windows and with its base lapped by the waves of the Seine, it soon became—as legend, Gaillardet, and Dumas would have it—the scene of nightly orgies indulged in by Queen Marguerite and her two sisters, Blanche and Jeanne.[24] Each morning the corpses of three handsome young noblemen—the lovers of the night before—washed ashore downstream from the tower ". . . because their eyes have seen what they should not have seen . . . because their lips have given and received kisses that they should neither have given nor received."

In the tavern of Orsini near the Porte St.-Honoré, Philippe d'Aulnay—newly arrived in Paris to seek his brother Gaultier—meets another recent arrival, a bold and mysterious man who calls himself Captain Buridan and who tells Philippe he shares a secret with Queen Marguerite that will either make his fortune or cause his death. Philippe confides that he has been given a rendezvous for that very night by a veiled lady; scarcely has he said so, however, when another veiled lady enters the tavern seeking Buridan and, in identical terms, makes a rendezvous with him. Despite the warnings of Gaultier d'Aulnay when he comes to find his brother, Philippe and Buridan set off for their unknown assignations.

It is, of course, to the Tour de Nesle that the new friends are both taken, and there they meet again later as they both attempt to escape. Marguerite, attracted to Philippe by his striking resemblance to Gaultier, the one man she truly loves, wishes to save him from the customary fate of her partners. For this reason she has not removed her mask; but Philippe, determined to know who she is, scratches her face through the mask with a pin so that he will be able to recognize her by the scar, thereby signing his death warrant. Buridan makes his escape by jumping into the river and swimming away, but Philippe is set upon by Marguerite's assassins and, just before he expires, Marguerite tears off her mask to let him see her face. "Marguerite of Burgundy!" he gasps. "Queen of France!" And as he sinks lifeless on the floor the curtain falls to the words of the night watchman outside: "Three o'clock and all's well. Sleep, Parisians."

The second act brings two confrontations between the queen and Buridan. The first occurs in the palace, with Buridan disguised as a gypsy soothsayer who terrifies Marguerite into accepting a rendezvous at Orsini's tavern by asking her if she was not surprised that this morning only two bodies had appeared in the Seine instead of three. The second is their subsequent meeting in the tavern. There, dressed again in his own clothes, Buridan blackmails the queen into writing orders for the arrest and execution of her first minister and the appointment of Buridan to the post. He can produce, he says, a note from Philippe, written in his own blood and accusing Marguerite of his murder. But Marguerite's vengeance begins only moments after Buridan's departure. She tricks Gaultier D'Aulnay into giving her Philippe's note, which he has been holding—unread—for Buridan. Once it is in her hands she orders

Buridan's immediate incarceration in the prison of the Grand Châtelet. Buridan's unexpectedly calm acceptance of Marguerite's triumph provides a stunning curtain and prepares the way for the ensuing prison scene.

Marguerite comes to Buridan's cell to gloat over his defeat, and here the clash between royal authority and the force of genius that Dumas saw as central to the play is developed most fully and explicitly. Marguerite taunts Buridan, burns Philippe's note in his presence, announces the imminent arrival of priest and executioner. Asked at last if he has something to say, Buridan quietly starts to tell his story. "In 1293, twenty years ago now,[25] Burgundy was happy," he begins, "for she was ruled by the beloved Duke Robert II . . ." Robert had a daughter Marguerite—"with the appearance of an angel, the soul of a devil"—and a young page, Lyonnet de Bourneville, who became lovers. When her father learned that she was pregnant he ordered her to a convent, but Marguerite prevailed upon Lyonnet to kill the duke. The day after the murder a man named Orsini delivered to the page a bag of gold and a letter in which, "because of their mutual crime," he was advised to leave the province for their mutual safety. The page left indeed, but had preserved the letter; a faithful friend was charged with delivering it to the king of France should anything untoward happen to the former page, now known as Buridan. And what was the fate of the twin sons she had borne him, Buridan now asks. The same Orsini, Marguerite replies, who had brought the letter to Lyonnet had been ordered to kill them; but, unable to bring himself to the act, had given them to a friend who had left them as foundlings at a church.

The queen is now once more in Buridan's power, and satisfaction of his ambition is again within his grasp. Marguerite herself unties his bonds, and the next day—under his real name of Lyonnet de Bourneville—he is recognized as first minister by the king. But if his ambition is realized, he still seeks vengeance on Marguerite and on Gaultier, who had betrayed him (or so he believes) by giving Philippe's note to Marguerite. Using his new authority he orders guardsmen to go to the Tower of Nesle that night and arrest whomever they find there, then contrives a rendezvous there between Gaultier and Marguerite. She, at the same time, is arranging an ambush there for Buridan. Waiting for events to take their course, Buridan questions Orsini's henchman about events in the past and discovers, to his horror, that Philippe and Gaultier d'Aulnay are his and Marguerite's long lost sons. Hastening to the tower to tell Marguerite what he has learned, Buridan arrives too late to prevent the murder of Gaultier by Orsini's and Marguerite's hired assassins, but just in time to fall—with Marguerite—victim to the trap he himself had prepared. This night there will be no escape from the Tower of Nesle.

Lust, adultery, incest, murder, and filicide—it would be hard to imagine a more extensive catalog of violence and crime contained within five acts or a swifter series of intrigues, counterintrigues, and coincidences jammed into the same space. But if, on reflection, the coincidences seem more contrived, the improbabilities even more improbable, it is the very speed with which they are piled on one another that makes us accept them. Dumas's unquestionable strength, says André Le Breton,[26] is precisely that he does not give us time to reflect. The flaws and contrivance that so leap to the eye when one looks back at the play, or reads it thoughtfully, simply do not count when, as spectator, one is carried along by the rush of the action.

For action dominates, as it should in melodrama, and *La Tour de Nesle* surely represents melodrama in its purest form. Dumas here no longer makes even a gesture toward historical realism (much less accuracy), nor toward the artistic seriousness implied by tragedy—though it would most certainly be a mistake to assume that he did not take his subject or his play seriously. He is dealing in *La Tour de Nesle* with legend, not fact, and with characters transformed or invented by legend. The historical framework provides color and atmosphere; it serves, as he says in the preface to *Catherine Howard* (1834), as "a nail on which I have hung my picture." And his picture is delineated in swift, serviceable prose—full of medieval oaths and exclamation points—that hurries the action along. The slower cadence of verse, its invitation to the listener to concern himself with other things than what is going to happen next, would only be out of place here. The play is frankly written for a popular audience by a man who knows what such an audience wants. A public nurtured on Gothic novels and on the melodramas of such successful writers as Pixérécourt went to the theater not for edification, not to be moved by noble or gorgeously colored poetry, but to be entertained, to be thrilled by the exploits of heroes and the horrors perpetrated by villains who ultimately (but never too soon!) receive their just deserts. The popular element always present in Dumas's plays here is central, unconcealed, and unabashed.

But though one may argue whether melodrama is art, there is nonetheless a kind of art in this particular melodrama; and it is this art that makes the play really Dumas's, whoever is credited with the original idea. The two scenes that we know are entirely Dumas's— the opening *tableau* and the prison scene—are indispensable additions. They give the whole drama its shape, they provide essential exposition without which both suspense and the clarity or motivation of subsequent events would suffer, and they unify the play by focussing the action on one explicitly presented conflict. The colors of period and place are also applied by Dumas with great skill. Details of language and allusion are carefully prevented from distracting by excess, and the Tower of Nesle itself becomes a tangible presence in the play. Only two of the play's nine scenes actually occur within it (I, 2 and V, 2), yet it casts its long and ominous shadow over the entire work, as what happens there determines or affects everything that happens elsewhere. The tower takes on, at one and the same time, the force of a living character— not unlike the cathedral in Hugo's *Notre-Dame de Paris*— and that of a symbol, the mute and terrifying symbol of the unnamable evil it harbors.

In the domain of character, too, Dumas's achievement is significant, though again in a way consistent with melodrama. The characters are not realistic. They are the product neither of subtle psychological analysis nor of careful observation of manners. But they are alive. However outlandish they and their actions at times may seem, we cannot help being interested in what they do and believing in them as they frenziedly work out their destiny. Further, they become types. As Antony stood for the individual against society and its conventions, so Buridan could be seen in 1832 as the individual against the forces of tyranny and political authority, in a conflict that was then very much alive. Or one might find in Buridan, as many a critic since Parigot has done, the first in the long line of Dumas's adventurer-heroes, men of action and soldiers of fortune, that later will include the likes of d'Artagnan and the Bussy d'Amboise of *La Dame de Monsoreau*. Similarly, Marguerite may well be seen as the first—and most extreme—example of the equally long line of female monsters that Dumas will create. Yet what remains remarkable in them, as in their successors, is the way in which Dumas has managed to give them life, to impart to them something of his own intense vitality. Despite shallowness and exaggeration, oversimplification and improbability, they do attain a kind of reality.

The esthetically sensitive, those of refined or intellectual taste, may well be honestly repelled by the excesses and, ultimately, the falseness of *La Tour de Nesle*. But to the thousands of others who have filled halls to witness and cheer thousands of performances, *La Tour de Nesle* has offered what they sought in the theater. It was never intended to be temperate, refined, or true—to life or anything else, except itself. Many a melodrama has fallen short of what Dumas set out to do, and did, in this one. Enough have failed for his achievement, fairly viewed on its own terms, to be appreciated at its real worth today as in 1832.

V *Comedy:* Mademoiselle de Belle-Isle *and its Successors*

Although Dumas continued writing and collaborating on plays at a pace almost as frantic as that of the action in most of them, he did not attempt a full-length comedy until 1839. *Le Mari de la veuve (The Widow's Husband)*, a one-act prose comedy written jointly with Anicet Bourgeois and Durieu, had been produced at the Comédie-Française seven years before. Not unlike his early *vaudevilles*, this play is slight, conventional, and quite predictable, albeit amusing. One senses Dumas's hand in the polished development of the action and in the lively dialogue, which even today does not seem without verve; but this little comedy by no means represented a significant excursion into a genre new to Dumas. If it did not diminish his reputation through inferiority or failure, by the same token *Le Mari de la veuve* did not enlarge it either.

Mademoiselle de Belle-Isle, on the other hand, was a departure from the kind of play Dumas had been writing and it enhanced his reputation considerably. Without creating anything like the sensation provoked by *Henri III* or *Antony*, it enjoyed genuine success when produced and it settled into the repertory of the Comédie-Française for a period of sustained popularity that Dumas achieved with no other play except *La Tour de Nesle*. In less than forty years *Mademoiselle de Belle-Isle* received over four hundred performances there and was still in the active repertory at the end of the century.[27]

The plot, according to Henri Blaze de Bury,[28] was suggested by an unperformed one-act comedy by Léon Lhéri, who wrote under the pen name of "Brunswick." Though the characters and a few background events are historical, the main action is fictitious. At the beginning of the play, the marquise de Prie and the duc de Richelieu end a liaison that they had agreed from the start would be temporary. Amused that they have simultaneously arrived at the same attitude toward their affair, each confesses a new romantic interest. The marquise now favors the chevalier d'Aubigny, a young Breton whom she has recently had appointed to the King's Guard at Chantilly; Richelieu is attracted to Gabrielle de Belle-Isle, granddaughter of Fouquet, Louis XIV's celebrated minister of finance. Richelieu then announces the arrival at Chantilly of Mlle de Belle-Isle, "who comes from Brittany to seek a pardon for her father and brothers, who are prisoners in the Bastille." The marquise agrees to use her influence with the duc de Bourbon to aid Mlle de Belle-Isle.

Two other noblemen, the chevalier d'Auvray and the duc d'Aumont arrive, followed shortly by the chevalier d'Aubigny. Challenged to prove that he is still the ladies' man he is reputed to be, the duc de Richelieu bets the others that he can seduce, within twenty-four hours, the next woman who enters the room. Not unexpectedly, the "victim" turns out to be Gabrielle de Belle-Isle. After she passes through, the chevalier d'Aubigny steps forward and challenges the duke to make good his bet, because ". . . in three days I am to marry the lady that M. le duc de Richelieu expects to dishonor within twenty-four hours."

The second act continues in the same vein, like the first reminiscent of Beaumarchais in deftly handled complications of plot, mistaken identities, and swift alterations of plans when events go awry. The duke tells the marquise about his bet and asks her assistance in winning it. The marquise pretends to agree but, by now secretly irked at the duke's prompt recovery from the end of their liaison, decides to foil him. First she invites Mlle de Belle-Isle to stay with her, then informs the duke of the room his prey will occupy. Arranging for Gabrielle to be transported to the Bastille for a visit with her father that very night, the marquise swears her to

secrecy about the trip and tells her that her father's fate—as well as
the marquise's—depends on absolute silence.

Tormented by his knowledge of the duke's bet and by Gabrielle's
anticipatory happiness—which she, of course, refuses to explain—
the chevalier d'Aubigny lurks on the premises to see what will
happen. Like the duke, he sees Mme de Prie's carriage depart at 10
o'clock and assumes that she is inside it, while she is, in reality,
waiting in Gabrielle's darkened room. The duke gains entry to the
chamber through a secret door. Confident that he has won his bet,
he tosses a prepared note announcing his success through the
window—to the waiting d'Aubigny, whom he mistakes for a
watchman. "Mademoiselle de Belle-Isle is alone here now,"
Richelieu gloats, *"Allons!"*

Dumas calls *Mademoiselle de Belle-Isle* a drama rather than a
comedy; beginning with the third act this designation seems more
valid. The light tone and the wit that dominate the first two acts do
not disappear completely, but they become more subdued as the
situation takes a more serious turn, the dialogue and confrontations
become more urgent, and a happy outcome seems less sure. The
opening scene between Gabrielle and d'Aubigny the next morning,
for example, verges on the bitterly ironic, if not exactly the tragic:
Gabrielle, sworn to secrecy, is helpless to explain her absence
overnight or to prove her innocence when d'Aubigny supports his
accusations with the duke's note. The traditional comic device of a
dialogue before a concealed witness whose presence is known only
to one of the participants similarly takes on a more ambiguous
coloration in the subsequent episode, when the duc de Richelieu,
convinced of his amorous success of the night before, only frustrates
Gabrielle's attempts to demonstrate her innocence to the listening
d'Aubigny. A final, more violent confrontation between Gabrielle
and d'Aubigny ends the act, as the young man storms out vowing
never to pardon his fiancée and the heartbroken Gabrielle prays for
heaven's pity.

The fourth act is a rapid and mounting succession of startling
events. The duc de Richelieu tells his story to the marquise de Prie,
who does not yet reveal what really happened. D'Aubigny
challenges Richelieu to a duel that is, however, prevented by the
intervention of a representative of the king. Still obsessed with the
apparent affront to his honor and that of Mademoiselle de Belle-Isle,
d'Aubigny then gambles with Richelieu to see which of them will

commit suicide as an alternative resolution of the situation. D'Aubigny loses. Just after he departs to end his life, word arrives that the duc de Bourbon and his favorite, Mme de Prie, have both been exiled by the king. The truth about the marquise's deception of Richelieu is accidentally revealed, but just as Richelieu prepares to leave and save d'Aubigny's life by setting matters straight, he too is arrested in the name of the king.

Coming to bid farewell to Gabrielle before his suicide, d'Aubigny mentions to her that the duc de Bourbon is no longer minister and that her protectress has also fallen out of royal favor. Thus freed from her promise to Mme de Prie, Gabrielle tells d'Aubigny about her nocturnal visit to the Bastille. When the voice of Richelieu is heard on the stair, Gabrielle hides in the next room, listens to the duke's apologies to d'Aubigny, then emerges and, on a note of happy reconciliation, the play ends.

As with Dumas's earlier triumphs in the theater, the immediate success of *Mademoiselle de Belle-Isle* was due at least in part to its timeliness. Once more he had sensed what would most please his audience and what would speak most directly to its tastes and current temper. Though the failure of Hugo's *Les Burgraves*—a failure that for a century or more has represented for literary historians the "official" demise of the Romantic drama—was still some four years off, there were already signs that the public was growing weary of the genre. Passions had been torn to tatters and the ears of the groundlings split long enough. The battle of Romanticism had been won nearly a decade before. Already, in 1838, Rachel had revived public appreciation of the majesty and restraint of Classical tragedy. And, just a week after the première of *Mademoiselle de Belle-Isle,* that of *L'Alchimiste (The Alchemist)*—a verse drama set in sixteenth century Italy that Dumas and Gérard de Nerval had written during their travels in Germany—was a failure. *Mademoiselle de Belle-Isle* is a better play than *L'Alchimiste,* but the magic name of Dumas had sufficed for the success of worse ones before; there can be no doubt that much of the warmth with which the public welcomed *Mademoiselle de Belle-Isle* was a response to its more civilized passions, its engaging characters, and a plot that managed to sacrifice violence and a tragic outcome without sacrificing interest. Charm and grace were refreshing after so many years of shock and relentless intensity.

Dumas did not cease being Dumas, however, though he had

studied his eighteenth century models well. The first two acts and the beginning of the fourth move on a web of bright and sometimes brittle repartee that often calls Marivaux and Beaumarchais to mind, though Dumas never quite equals the spontaneous wit and light, easy grace of the former or the social and psychological penetration of the latter. The conventional elements of eighteenth century comedy are there: the marquise's clever servant-confidante; symmetrical episodes like the parallel scenes with a concealed listener; mixed identities and intricate plotting. The atmosphere of the Regency period perfumes the whole work also: naive innocence contrasted with worldly sophistication, the relaxed morality of the aristocracy, the ever-present menace of royal disfavor (and the Bastille) that hovers in the shadows while pleasures as entrancing as they are temporary glitter in center stage. But despite his effective use of all these devices, Dumas is still most successful where he always has been. The familiar touch is present in the muted but real tension of the dramatic moments, in the steady build-up of action, in the unerring sense of when and on what line to ring down the curtain. For all his natural verve and good humor, for all the cleverness and wit he is able to inject into his comedies, Dumas's essential theatrical genius is dramatic, not comic.

Mademoiselle de Belle-Isle was favorably received by critics as well as by actors and public. Even Sainte-Beuve, usually so critical of Dumas, professed admiration,[29] though he was also perhaps the first to point out the striking improbability on which the action is based. In the cold light of day—or even in the dark of Mme de Prie's bedchamber—it is indeed difficult to believe that an experienced roué would not have realized the trick being played on him by his ex-mistress. But accept it the playgoers did, and Sainte-Beuve with them in the end. It is a tribute to the dramatist's sure control that his play neither foundered on this hazardous reef nor caught in the shoals of melodrama that it skimmed past so closely. Precisely because of its combination of shrewd theatricality, lively charm, and avoidance of exaggerated effects *Mademoiselle de Belle-Isle* would probably better than most of Dumas's plays bear production today. While its sparkle might prove to be somewhat faded and its heroine a trifle prissy, it would surely appear less dated (though also, perhaps, less important) than an *Antony*.

Two years later Dumas repeated the initial success, if not the long-range popularity, of *Mademoiselle de Belle-Isle* with another comedy in the eighteenth century style, *Un Mariage sous Louis XV* (*A Marriage of Convenience*). The plot is slight and familiar. A marriage of convenience is arranged between the Comte de Candale and a girl just coming out of a convent, Mlle de Torigny. Each enters into the marriage willingly but with heart admittedly elsewhere. The action consists of the various steps by which the young count and countess discover at the end, to no one else's great surprise, that they have fallen in love with each other.

F. W. Reed states categorically that "This is decidedly Dumas's finest and most witty full-length comedy."[30] Even though Dumas wrote only three "full-length" (i.e., five-act) comedies, this judgment requires qualification. The play is indeed witty, in manner as well as dialogue. It is, if anything, more neatly constructed and more perfectly put together than *Mademoiselle de Belle-Isle;* there is, for example, no problem of an underlying *invraisemblance* that the audience must be made to accept. The style of the eighteenth century is as well achieved as in the earlier play and the comic tone is as well sustained. The form of the typical comedy of psychological analysis is masterfully reproduced. Where Dumas reveals his limitations is precisely in the play's superficial perfection. As Parigot observes most aptly, "never was contrivance more obvious nor skill so irritating."[31] Charm, wit, style, invention are all there, but the careful symmetry of structure tends toward predictability, and Dumas's characters play their roles gracefully without ever revealing the secret intimacies of their hearts and minds as do Marivaux's heroes and heroines or those of Dumas's contemporary, Musset. We must concur with Parigot that here the skill of the theatrical craftsman underscores the inadequacies of the psychologist. If it seems unrealistic or unfair to demand such penetration of Dumas, it must be remembered that illuminating observation of character is the one indispensable element of a *comédie d'analyse,* no matter how well everything else may be done. That Dumas succeeds to the extent he does in *Un Mariage sous Louis XV* is yet another demonstration of his theatrical gifts. That the success is less than total merely shows that here he is not *dans son genre.*

About *Les Demoiselles de Saint-Cyr* (*The Girls of Saint-Cyr*), a third comedy in similar vein, much the same can be said. The action takes place in 1700, and one of the protagonists is Mme de Maintenon; but again Dumas relies more on situations than on

exploration of character, more on artificial symmetry of structure
and contrast of personalities than on inner motivations in order to
carry his play along and to provide the comic or touching effects he
seeks. Less successful than either *Mademoiselle de Belle-Isle* or *Un
Mariage sous Louis XV* when first produced, *Les Demoiselles de
Saint-Cyr* is a more uneven play in style as well as substance,
though it still has its champions and, up to 1892, had more
performances (226) at the Comédie-Française than any other play by
Dumas except *Mademoiselle de Belle-Isle*.[32] Today its chief claim to
interest may well be the fact that it was selected by Queen Victoria
to be performed for her during the royal visit to Paris in 1855.[33]

Halifax (1842), a comedy-drama with a hero reminiscent of
Figaro; four other one-act comedies; and two more *opéra-comique*
librettos (including *Le Roman d'Elvire*, done in collaboration with
Adolphe de Leuven) complete the list of Dumas's attempts at comic
writing for the theater. Despite his native exuberance and sense of
humor Dumas was, on the whole, less at home with comedy as a
theatrical genre than with most others, yet these plays deserve to be
better known than they are. They reveal a significant, if limited,
aspect of his work as a dramatist and in their own right possess both
interest and charm.

CHAPTER 3

The Dramatist: Development and Evaluation

I Tangents and Permutations

BETWEEN 1829 and the end of 1851, when Dumas began his voluntary exile in Brussels, only one year—1844—saw no new play by him on some Parisian stage.[1] Several years saw four or five produced, and in April of 1839 he actually achieved three premières within fifteen days. One of these was *Mademoiselle de Belle-Isle*, and it would not be unfair to say that this success both climaxed and closed the important decade of Dumas's career as a playwright. Though he continued to turn out plays at a frequently astounding rate and to draw enthusiastic crowds until the year before his death, after *Mademoiselle de Belle-Isle* Dumas's most original and influential plays were behind him. One might also add "his best," as no later play, whatever its merits, surpassed the best plays of the 1830's either in quality or importance.

The year before *Mademoiselle de Belle-Isle* Dumas had for the first time drawn a play—*Paul Jones*—from one of his own novels. Increasingly this was to be his procedure. After *Les Demoiselles de Saint-Cyr* almost all his new plays were dramatizations or reworkings of the materials of his enormously popular novels and romances. Some twenty of the sixty-six plays included in the Michel Lévy edition of the *Théâtre complet* fall into this category, while from the period 1843–1849 only *Catalina* and *Le Comte Hermann* do not. Many of these adaptations were as theatrically effective as they were successful in performance—e.g., *La Reine Margot*, which opened Dumas's Théâtre Historique in 1847, holding its audience enthralled from 6 P.M. until 3 o'clock the next morning, or the first two of the four plays needed to translate *The Count of Monte-Cristo* to the stage. For reasons as obvious as those leading Dumas to write them, however, these plays cannot be read or evaluated in the same way as his others.[2]

But even before thus making his subjects and plots do double duty, Dumas had not been a man to abandon a vein once discovered until he was sure it had been exhausted. Seeming to explore all possible genres and turning from one to another with every fluctuation of public taste or his own fancy, he always maintained a steady flow of works in patterns or styles that he found successful. The obvious example, as we have seen, is the series of three Regency comedies that began with *Mademoiselle de Belle-Isle*. Actually, each of his early successes led to further plays of similar type; even *Christine* inspired one further verse tragedy—*Charles VII chez ses grands vassaux* (*Charles the Seventh and his Great Vassals*). Works without any counterpart elsewhere in Dumas's *oeuvre*, such as *Don Juan de Marana* (1836) and *Le Vampire* (1851), were usually dubious successes at best and of even more dubious quality.

The richest veins that Dumas exploited were the two genres that he created, the historical drama and the modern drama. *Henri III et sa cour*, asserts Parigot,[3] has no direct successors among Dumas's plays. Within Parigot's categories this is true: in none of the subsequent historical tragedies, dramas, or comedies does Dumas—whatever his inaccuracies here—work as directly from historical sources, strive so hard to stay within the limits they impose, or so truly achieve a *drame national populaire*. Long before he described *Catherine Howard* (1834) as a *"drame extra-historique"* he had strayed far from his goals in *Henri III*. But, in a larger sense, all of Dumas's historical plays are progeny of *Henri III et sa cour* because there he learned how to bring a remote era to life, to shape history into colorful, concrete dramatic form—or, more precisely, to extract the colors of history and apply them to his dramatic structures.

The offspring of *Antony*, generally more individual and distinctive than those of *Henri III*, are also far less numerous. As designated by Dumas, there are at best half as many *drames modernes* as there are *drames historiques*. The first in time and the best known are *Richard Darlington* (1831), *Teresa* (1832), *Angèle* (1833), and *Kean* (1836); among the later ones, *Le Comte Hermann* (1849) was a particular favorite of Dumas's. A sentimental and now sadly dated play set in Germany, its preface—one of the few Dumas wrote—is of more interest today than the play itself.

Richard Darlington is a melodrama of passion, ambition, and politics. The hero, like Antony, is illegitimate, though his father is known to the audience from the beginning and his illegitimacy is considerably less central to the action than is the case in the earlier play. Richard is a young man totally without scruples and devoured by ambition. When his election to Parliament is threatened because of the obscurity of his origins, he promptly acquires family and connections through marriage to Jenny, daughter of Richard's widely respected guardian, Dr. Grey. Successful and influential as Sir Richard, M.P., he keeps Jenny sequestered in the country while he passes himself off in London as a bachelor. When the possibility arises of an advantageous marriage (to the adopted daughter of his real but unknown mother), he asks Jenny for a divorce. Jenny refuses, so Richard arranges for her to be abducted and taken to France, while the records of their marriage in England are to be destroyed. Richard's father (now known as Mawbray) intervenes to save Jenny, but when Richard finds her at his country house— where he has come to meet his future in-laws—they quarrel violently and he pushes her off a balcony to her death. Before the marriage agreements can be signed, however, Mawbray intervenes again. This time he reveals his true identity—the executioner, as well as Richard's father—thus destroying the plans of his ruthless son.

Behind the obvious differences in setting and theme, certain fundamental resemblances between *Richard Darlington* and *Antony* can be perceived. In each case a hero whose birth is shrouded in mystery engages in a solitary struggle against the obstacles society has placed in the way of successful attainment of the goals he seeks. Richard's selfish ambition, manifested in his drive for political power, wealth, and status, is as intense and single-minded as Antony's passion for Adèle. Correspondingly, the hapless heroines both become victims of the men they love, though Antony kills Adèle because he loves her but cannot have her, while Richard kills Jenny because he has her and does not want her. In the course of both plays the specific social forces—moral conventions, political exigencies—that frustrate the heroes come under attack directly and through satire. On a deeper level, a final parallel emerges as an irony: despite the hero's revolt, however justified it might seem, the values of the society he rejects are sustained and ultimately triumphant.[4] In contrast to the heroes, each of the heroines is squarely on the side of society as it is constituted. Adèle defends its demands on her (*Antony*, Act II, scene 5) and Jenny in her conventionality wins our sympathy and respect as her husband never does. Further, each of the heroes at least tacitly acknowledges his error as he finally submits to the will of society.

Teresa and *Angèle* followed close on the heels of *Richard Darlington* and, like it, reveal a generic consistency beneath apparently greater external differences. In the first of these plays, Teresa, brought back from Naples as the bride of the Baron Delaunay, finds her new step-daughter Amélie engaged to Arthur de Savigny whom she, Teresa, had known and loved in Italy. Arthur marries Amélie but he and Teresa eventually succumb to their rekindled passion and become lovers. The baron discovers the truth and, though appalled, arranges things to preserve appearances for the sake of all four parties. Teresa, however, unable to live with her sin and shame, commits suicide.

Though a considerable success with the public in 1832, *Teresa* is a rather weak play, of interest chiefly because here the protagonist, the individual whose passions are frustrated by society, is a woman. Many of the social questions raised in *Antony* are again raised here—the status of women, the problem of adultery, the reputation of a wife and her husband's honor, the right of an individual to sacrifice convention to passion—and again the resolution is characterized by ironic ambiguity. Though Teresa earns our sympathy in her illicit but overpowering love for Arthur, she is intended also to win our admiration by her submission and self-punishment in the name of society and conventional morality.

Angèle, to some extent a variation on the themes of *Teresa*, is a better constructed and generally stronger play. The central character (despite the implication of the title) is once again a man; and, where Antony embodied passion and Richard Darlington ambition, Alfred d'Alvimar in this play is Dumas's most successful example of the Don Juan—much more so, certainly, than the protagonist of *Don Juan de Marana*, Dumas's "official" play on the subject and probably the worst he ever wrote.

The play opens in the Pyrenees, where the rake Alfred d'Alvimar seduces the innocent young Angèle, then runs off to Paris with her widowed but still young and attractive mother. Nine months later Angèle arrives at her mother's home in Paris to have her baby, just as d'Alvimar is preparing to abandon the mother and go off to Germany. When she learns the truth, Angèle's mother insists that d'Alvimar marry her daughter at once. He tries to escape but is prevented from doing so by Henri Muller, a virtuous young man—actually Angèle's doctor—who has long loved her in silence and followed her to Paris from the Pyrenees. Henri challenges d'Alvimar to a duel and kills him, then claims the expected child as his and prepares to marry Angèle, though he knows he is dying of consumption.

Once again the self-seeking protagonist is defeated, but this time his innocent victim is saved. The sentimental tone of *Angèle*, which it shares with *Teresa*, is both more pronounced and more sustained than the sentimentality in *Richard Darlington*, where it was much more episodic, or in *Antony*, where it was largely inundated by more intense and violent feeling. If this represents a change, however, *Angèle* still has in common with *Richard Darlington* a thoroughly unpleasant central male character, a genuine anti-hero who, like Richard (and Antony before him), places himself and his values in opposition to society and its demands. When, as here, the opponent of society does not engage our sympathy, the punishment that follows the rebellion seems more consistent, less ambiguous, but the essential conflict of individual and society is still there at the heart of the drama.

Called a comedy by Dumas and characterized by considerable humor and a happy ending, *Kean* is nonetheless traditionally and appropriately classed among the *drames modernes*. Like them it relates to a period that could still be called contemporary by an audience in 1836; more importantly, its subject and development are essentially serious. Its theme, beloved of many Romantics, is the alienation of the artist from society. Alfred de Vigny had treated it only a year earlier in his *Chatterton*. Given Dumas's propensity for seizing upon fashionable subjects it would be easy to attribute *Kean* to a desire to emulate Vigny's success, but apart from the general subject and the nationality of the heroes the two plays have nothing in common. The fact that Dumas's artist is an actor while Vigny's had been a poet further points up their significant differences.

Dumas's inspiration is much more likely to have been simply his own recollections of Kean's performances in Paris in 1827–28 and a desire to offer a tribute to the actor, recently deceased, whose portrayals of Shakespearean roles had so affected him as a young man.

The structure of *Kean* is particularly interesting and an excellent example of Dumas's inventiveness. As in *Antony,* the initial exposition is accomplished through a conversation between the heroine (in this case one of two leading female characters) and a confidante. Unlike *Antony* and the other dramas we have examined, however, *Kean* does not plunge the spectator into the midst of conflict and violent passions. The movement, without being slow, is relaxed and spacious. The hero appears at the start to have achieved everything he could hope for: fame, universal admiration for his acting genius, a discreet but positive response to the love he professes for Elena (wife of the Danish ambassador), and the esteem and friendship of the Prince of Wales. The play unfolds in a series of situations that explore, both naturally and dramatically, the reality of the actor's life behind these appearances.

Kean's genius sets him apart from the other players, *saltimbanques,* and popular entertainers from whose ranks he rose and whose affection he still retains. Yet his successive confrontations with Lord Mewill (whose scheme for the abduction of the young heiress Anna Damby is foiled by Kean), with the Prince of Wales, and with Elena herself all prove that his genius cannot bridge the other gap either—the one that separates him, as an actor, from the rest of society. Lord Mewill refuses to duel with Kean, his social inferior, and remains untouched by the law for his illegal actions because of his rank; the Prince of Wales reveals in several ways that his friendship for Kean, though sincere, cannot make them equals as real friends must be; and Elena, in the end, cannot sacrifice either her social status or the proffered love of the Prince of Wales for the sake of loving Kean. The play ends happily—Kean leaves for America with Anna Damby, whose love for him is sure—but the departure is in fact an exile. As in the other *drames modernes,* the hero, unsuccessful in his struggle against society's values, finally bows to them.

A number of the stock characters and situations of melodrama are present in *Kean,* but they do not dominate the play. The tone of the whole work is unusually subdued for Dumas, so that the one truly melodramatic scene—Act IV, tableau ii, scene 2, where Kean, playing Romeo,[5] challenges the Prince of Wales from the stage— projects tremendous excitement. This episode displays in powerfully dramatic fashion the contrasting sides of Kean's nature pointed out in the play's subtitle, *Disorder and Genius.* Its centrality demonstrates Dumas's preoccupation with character and theme in this play, as opposed to his customary emphasis on rapid action and plot development. This concern is further reflected in Dumas's unusual but apt use of long speeches and what are, in effect, soliloquies by Kean. Though the subject matter and intent are totally different, one hears a distant echo of Hamlet's advice to the players in Kean's long speech to Anna in Act II, when he advises her to abandon her dreams of being an actress; and the Prince of Denmark's shade hovers again in the background whenever his nineteenth century interpreter muses alone on his fate or on human nature and folly. It is a singularly effective device for both characterization and atmosphere.

Beyond Kean's dual nature, the opposition of terms in the subtitle—*Disorder and Genius*—further suggests the conflicts that mark his life on other levels. In Act IV, scene 2, Kean points out his personal dilemma: his dramatic genius could not flower in the context of an orderly personal life, free of his emotional (and alcoholic) excesses. The irony of his social dilemma lies also in the paradox of his genius, which earns him the admiration of the high-born and the wealthy yet which, by its nature, denies him full admittance to that order of society. Finally his human dilemma: the exceptional man is set apart from all his fellows by the very genius that enables him to speak to them most meaningfully. Though Kean leaves joyfully with Anna at the end, it is clear that none of these dilemmas, least of all the last, has been—or can ever be—fully resolved.

The foregoing should not suggest that in *Kean* philosophy dominates theater or that Dumas here achieves an unprecedented profundity. The ideas are indeed there and this play is distinctly more thoughtful and searching than virtually any of his others, but it remains a drama. Dumas makes full use of the opportunities offered by his subject for contrast of tone, mood, and movement. Kean is called upon to demonstrate a much greater range and variety of emotions than most Dumasian heroes, and the human

backgrounds—as well as the settings—against which he displays
them are no less kaleidoscopic. Once again Dumas proves that,
whatever his faults, he could not write an untheatrical play.

II *Dumas and the Theater*

Dumas ranks twentieth among authors performed at the
Comédie-Française, where eighteen of his plays have received a
total of 1820 performances.[6] Yet these figures represent only a tiny
fraction of the activity that made him the most popular playwright of
his day if not of his entire century. In this inconsistency lies a clue to
Dumas's nature as a dramatist and to his place in the nineteenth
century French theater.

Dumas enjoyed his first triumph at the Comédie-Française. He
can legitimately be credited with creating the Romantic historical
drama there in February, 1829, with *Henri III et sa cour,* and no
small part of his achievement that night was represented by the
stature of the house in which his play was performed. Most of his
subsequent successes, however, were staged not in that august hall,
but rather in the popular *théâtres des boulevards.* This was no
source of distress or disappointment to Dumas; quite the contrary.
However proud he was of his achievements in the strongholds of art,
he remained, equally proudly, a writer for the people. Though he
counted as friends the literary and artistic elite of the day, he wrote
less for them than for the new bourgeois theatergoing public
spawned by the Revolution. He never lost the simplicity of his own
humble beginnings, and because he did not lose touch with the
common man he rarely misjudged what would please him. If there
is a single constant in Dumas's theater and a single unifying
characteristic, it is its quality of popular appeal. Whatever
interested Dumas—and what did not?—found its way into his
writing and, with exceptional frequency, interested his public also.
Whether he was inspired by what was currently popular or whether
he helped to crystallize vague, half-formed tendencies is often
difficult to decide in specific instances. That he was keenly attuned
to the changing feelings, tastes, and aspirations of his epoch,
however, is beyond doubt, as he too was fully aware. In the preface
to *Le Comte Hermann* (1849) he wrote:

—Yes, I'll write a simple, intimate and passionate drama for you, like
Antony and like *Angèle;* only the passions will no longer be the same,

because the period we live in now is different, because the age at which I am writing is different, because I have lived through those passions I described then . . . .

If this acute sensitivity to the public fancy and the at times undiscriminating catholicity of his personal interests is the explanation for his continuing popular success, it also provides the basis for the only evolution really discernible in his theater. Little artistic maturation is evident in Dumas's plays as they are studied in sequence, and after *Kean* he makes no serious attempt at exploration of new genres except for *Mademoiselle de Belle-Isle* and the two succeeding Regency comedies. By the 1840's his theatrical output, though still enormous, takes a decidedly secondary place to the writing of novels. The creative energies are now channelled in another direction.

A second constant in Dumas's plays, including the adaptations of his later years, is his unfailing dramatic sense and inventiveness. Not only was he interested in everything, but he perceived everything in dramatic terms—events he witnessed, stories he heard, emotions he felt or observed. He had no conscious system. "Theater is above all a matter of fantasy," he wrote in the preface to *Charles VII chez ses grands vassaux.* "I cannot understand, therefore, how anyone can imprison it in a system." But if system was lacking, instinct and vision were abundant and all-powerful in translating all his ideas, all his responses into vivid and concrete drama. He seems often to think in scenes and curtain lines; the sudden perception of a dénouement, as with *Antony,* could be the germ of a whole play. Unquestionably this is his greatest gift—his special genius—as a playwright.

Style was not among his virtues, and his style has been criticized from his day to ours. Dumas himself admitted his deficiencies in this respect. For more than a century now critics have been pointing out his grammatical errors, pomposity, and awkwardness, as well as his naiveté or occasional downright silliness. All these defects can be found, of course, but when all is said and done they are neither the real measure of his achievement nor the essential qualities of his prose. He is a master of swift, to-the-point dialogue. The quick, unpretentious exchanges that fill his plays are, in almost every case, the most appropriate and effective means of saying what he wants to say and of maintaining the pace.

For more important than style per se in almost any play by Dumas is movement. Energy and vitality, intensity and impetuous speed are part of his style too. Perhaps, as Parigot has observed, they are its essence: "If drama is passion in action, Dumas's language is appropriately that of drama."[7] Dumas never intended his public to follow subtle character analysis or to savor exquisitely chiselled verse at leisure; the public for which he wrote was not, by and large, interested in such things and no one knew it better than he did. Dumas worked instead for broad effect; he did not paint miniatures. To borrow a phrase from Parigot again, he "painted on a large scale, to be seen from a distance, by candlelight."[8]

Lack of style and subtlety, of the more literary qualities, may well be at least a significant reason—if not the only one—for the failure of most of Dumas's plays to survive his century, as has recently been suggested.[9] A greater weakness in Dumas's theater, however, is his failure to create real and memorable characters whose humanity is universal enough to reach beyond the age in which they were conceived. Types there are, even archetypes such as Antony and Buridan; but it is only thus that we remember them, and rarely apart from the plays in which they live. Even the most striking of Dumas's theatrical heroes never step out from their dramatic contexts as individualized, as independent, or as likable as a d'Artagnan, a Chicot, or even certain minor figures in the best of the romances. But, like style, such characters also are perhaps inappropriately looked for in a theater which operated on a different scale, with different values.[10] If Dumas's plays, taken as a whole, are frankly melodramas, then it is in terms of melodrama that they must be judged—and as melodramas written for a particular society, with particular tastes, in a particular era. It has been argued, with justice, that good melodramas are not necessarily worse than bad tragedies.

Largely dead today—or at least unrevived—Dumas's plays still retain indisputable importance both in the history of the nineteenth century French theater and in Dumas's own career. *Henri III et sa cour* and *Antony* provided models for developing genres and, for good or ill, influenced playwrights (including Dumas's own son) for the better part of a century. *La Tour de Nesle* too engendered countless imitations. Dumas's popularity—in both senses of the word—likewise had a significant impact on the general direction followed by the French theater during his lifetime. And, in his own career, the theater provided both the springboard to fame and a training ground for the novelist whose books betray on almost every page their author's sense of drama.

CHAPTER 4

The Romancer of History

DUMAS came to the novel, as he had come to fame in the theater, through history. Except for his *Nouvelles contemporaines (Contemporary Tales)*, which sold only four copies in the year of their publication (1826), Dumas's first ventures into prose narrative were the *scènes historiques* that he published in the *Revue des Deux-Mondes* beginning in 1831. Expanding his aims, the following year he assembled his first "historical compilation," *Gaule et France;* some three years after that *Isabel de Bavière* introduced his *Chroniques de France,* based primarily on the writings of the great medieval chroniclers.

These works and their successors of the same type—Dumas produced them throughout his career—were not, however, viewed by him as fiction. Having "discovered" history, he wanted to share his discovery and he saw part of his mission as a writer to do so. "I have always wanted," he states in the introduction to *La Comtesse de Salisbury* (1838), "to devote a part of my artistic life to historical works (it is not a question here of my plays). . . ."[1]

His goal in these historical works, he continues, is to offer the reader an alternative to "history properly speaking"—the boring accumulation of dates and facts, a skeleton from which flesh and blood have been stripped away; to historical novels—which deform history and, unless they are written by a genius of the order of Scott, are only "magic lanterns without light, color or scope"; and to original chronicles—a rich and reliable source but one difficult of access because of archaic language and the masses of detail that obscure the grand design of events.

His solution is to choose the historical period and events that interest him, then to flesh out the skeleton by studying closely the personalities and passions that brought about the drama. The old chronicles are quoted freely for the color of the period as well as for livening details of character, and they provide hints for the dialogue that Dumas invents with equal freedom. No nonhistorical character is introduced, however. In this way essential historical truth is respected and "art is used only to follow the thread that, winding through the three levels of society, links events to each other."

But art soon does a bit more than merely "follow the thread," as Dumas's sense of the dramatic could not be satisfied by the routine task he had set himself. Further, it was the living drama he perceived in history that attracted him and that he really wanted to convey to his readers. Touches of the romancer begin to appear very soon in these ostensibly nonfictional works, though on the whole Dumas submits to the authority of his sources and his self-imposed principles. By the time of *La Comtesse de Salisbury*, if not already in *Isabel de Bavière*, he has consciously substituted "the form of the chronicle for that of the annal and abandoned chronological concision for development of the picturesque."

Indeed, *La Comtesse de Salisbury* momentarily blurs the distinction that Dumas himself had made between historical fiction and historical "compilation." While belonging to his series of *Chroniques de France*—for that purpose covering the period 1338–77—it was his first work to be published as a serial novel and is generally viewed as such by literary historians. Like *Acté*, which Dumas published the following year (1839) and called a novel, it is largely a patchwork of materials drawn directly from chronicles and histories, all rather loosely and awkwardly cast in novel form. Such uncertainty of form and method, however, is not surprising at this stage in Dumas's development.

The years 1837–43 may fairly be viewed as an apprenticeship. Dumas's creative energies and interest are now more and more channelled toward fiction conceived as such, while he gradually develops the craft and form that will produce his most characteristic and enduring works. As he becomes more sure of himself his novels become more personal and assured. He *uses* his sources more than he simply follows them. Strict chronology yields to compression or alteration of events for dramatic effect; action and—especially—dialogue increasingly supplant narration; and Dumas's conceptions of his characters enlarge, if they do not alter, the givens of history. The novels now become distinct in manner as well as intent from the historical compilations, which pursue their original course, often—as in the case of *Louis XIV et son siècle (Louis the Fourteenth and his*

Century), published the same year as Les Trois Mousquetaires—
running parallel to the fictional creations.

These years of apprenticeship are also a time when Dumas,
despite the celebrity attached to his name, is to some degree
seeking a new audience. His fortunes in the theater during this
period slump, only Mademoiselle de Belle-Isle being really
successful while several other plays are outright failures. His many
volumes of impressions de voyage attract a certain public, but a
limited one, as is true also of such works as his Chroniques de
France, the early novels, and even the series of Crimes célèbres
(Famous Crimes), which clearly aimed its popularized accounts of
the nefarious deeds of the Borgias, the Marquise de Brinvilliers, the
Cenci, and others of their ilk at a sensation-seeking mass audience.

The audience that Dumas found, as Frédéric Soulié and Eugène
Sue had before him, was composed of the avid readers of romans-
feuilletons. These serial novels, introduced in the mid-1830's as a
means of increasing circulation of the new low-priced newspapers,
grew steadily in popularity, bringing wider fame and higher fees to
successful authors as well as more subscribers to the journals.
Beginning in 1838 Dumas contributed to four of them: La Presse, Le
Journal des Débats, Le Siècle, and Le Constitutionnel. (To this list
later were added the journals he himself founded.) Though Dumas
was immediately successful as a feuilletonniste, he was by no means
the overnight sensation he had been as author of Henri III et sa
cour. Four or five years of modest successes and experiments in
various genres were needed before he found his way.

Le Chevalier d'Harmental (1842), his first novel done in
collaboration with Auguste Maquet, established Dumas as a novelist
and pointed the direction he was to follow. A story based on events
surrounding the conspiracy of Cellamare during the Regency, it
successfully combined history, intrigue, high adventure, and
romance in a manner soon to become familiar to thousands of
readers the world over. It was well received, if not with unanimous
enthusiasm, and was reprinted in book form the year after its
appearance as a serial. Today critical opinion remains divided about
it. For Henri Clouard it is the work of a master. "Never," he states
categorically, "did Dumas surpass this achievement in historical
interpretation and balance between history and the novel." Gilbert
Sigaux, on the other hand, dismisses it equally categorically as
"without a spark."[2] Whether the reader shares one of these extreme

views or takes a position somewhere in between, he cannot deny the importance of *Le Chevalier d'Harmental* in Dumas's *oeuvre* and in his career. With this book Dumas found his pattern and actually began the series of novels embracing three centuries of French history on which his greatest fame rests. He was approaching the peak of his powers as a novelist when he wrote it; after it he was ready to embark on the prodigious decade during which he exploited those powers to the full.

In 1844 Dumas published five novels and began serial publication of a sixth. Four of these novels—*Amaury, Sylvandire, Gabriel Lambert,* and *Fernande*—are not without merit or interest, but they pale or disappear in the blaze of the other two. Only Dumas could outdo Dumas, and he did in that year. Between 1829 and 1831 Dumas had created two new dramatic genres, the *drame historique* with *Henri III et sa cour* and the *drame moderne* with *Antony*. In 1844 he produced *Les Trois Mousquetaires* and began publishing *Le Comte de Monte-Cristo*.

CHAPTER 5

The d'Artagnan Trilogy

I   Les Trois Mousquetaires

IF Dumas had written nothing but *The Three Musketeers* his fame would have been assured. Certainly no other work of his is better known and certainly none has surpassed it in consistent and widespread popularity. It remains also, as a total achievement, Dumas's finest novel. For this last reason, especially, it is almost an inevitable choice for the reader who wishes not only to sample Dumas's storytelling at its best but to examine the way he uses historical materials and builds a novel.

The familiar story begins on a day in April, 1625, in the town of Meung-sur-Loire. A young Gascon—"a Don Quixote at eighteen"—arrives astride a weary yellow nag, wearing his father's long sword and carrying fifteen *écus* and a letter of introduction to M. de Tréville, captain of the King's Musketeers in Paris. A stranger's insulting remark about his horse rouses d'Artagnan's Gascon temper and leads to a fight in which the stranger's henchmen quickly overpower d'Artagnan. The unknown offender—later identified as the comte de Rochefort, right-hand man of Cardinal Richelieu—is glimpsed by d'Artagnan in conversation with the beautiful and equally mysterious "Milady." Some time after their precipitate departure d'Artagnan discovers that his letter to M. de Tréville has been stolen. He arrives in the capital without further misadventure, sells his horse, finds lodging and, at the end of Chapter I, prepares to call on M. de Tréville.

At M. de Tréville's *hôtel* d'Artagnan meets successively Porthos, Aramis, and Athos, fights them successively in duels, then joins them to turn back an attack by the cardinal's guards. The friendship of the four is sealed and King Louis XIII, impressed by d'Artagnan's bravery, appoints him to his personal guard. The young man, however, retains his dream of someday belonging to the elite corps of Musketeers.

Through his charming young landlady, Constance Bonacieux, who is coincidentally a lady-in-waiting to the queen, Anne of Austria, d'Artagnan and his friends become involved in the affair of the queen's diamonds. The English ambassador, the Duke of Buckingham, is in love with the queen; she returns his affection and gives him, when he returns to England, a set of twelve diamond studs previously given to her by the king. Cardinal Richelieu, learning of the gift and jealous of the queen's preference for Buckingham, commissions Milady to steal two of the studs. When Milady succeeds, Richelieu contrives to have the king request his wife to wear all of them at a forthcoming ball. A top-speed trip to England by d'Artagnan—ambushes en route prevent his comrades from reaching and crossing the Channel with him—and duplication of the missing studs by Buckingham's jeweler save the day for the queen. In gratitude, she discreetly gives d'Artagnan a diamond ring.

The next section of the book alternates in a kind of counterpoint the dark activities of Milady and her lover de Wardes with the humorous exploits of Porthos and his courtship of Mme Coquenard, a *procureur*'s wife. D'Artagnan becomes entangled in the doings of Milady and, in the famous episode where he replaces de Wardes at an amorous rendezvous, he discovers the brand on her shoulder that mutely witnesses to her criminal past. Her identity is fully revealed in succeeding chapters.

Richelieu offers a post in his personal guard to d'Artagnan, but the Gascon declines. His sole ambition remains to become a musketeer, an ambition that is finally realized as a consequence of his bravery in the course of the next major episode of the book, the siege of La Rochelle. As Richelieu's agent, Milady has her role in this section too, eventually sailing to England to arrange for the assassination of Buckingham. After the half-comic, half-heroic defense of the Bastion Saint-Gervais, the musketeers—now four—are off again to foil her plotting. Warned by them of her return to England and its purpose, Milady's brother-in-law, Lord de Winter, imprisons her. She subverts her young guard, John Felton, however, incites him to murder Buckingham, and then escapes to France.

In the concluding section of the novel Milady and Rochefort meet at the convent in Béthune where Richelieu has had Constance Bonacieux concealed. Arriving to rescue Constance, the musketeers force the plotters to flee, but not before Milady manages to poison her. This last crime is too much; the musketeers overtake Milady and, supported by de Winter, exact their grim vengeance. The tragic tone of the end is somewhat mitigated by d'Artagnan's winning the friendship of Richelieu and a lieutenancy in the Musketeers. Porthos and Aramis leave the military life, the former to marry the recently widowed Mme Coquenard, the latter to enter holy orders. Athos remains a musketeer, but after a few years retires to country life in Roussillon.

Such a brief summary can only suggest the richness of incident in the novel and cannot convey at all the liveliness of its telling, but even a résumé makes immediately apparent the place of history in *Les Trois Mousquetaires*. Far from being a mere backdrop, it forms the very fabric of the tale. Widely known historical events provide the basis for important actions in the novel just as history supplies its major characters. But secondary episodes and less prominent characters are also grounded in fact. The siege of La Rochelle and the assassination of the Duke of Buckingham, for example, are immediately recognizable historical realities. But the story of the queen's diamonds which dominates the first half of the book, though seeming too fantastic to be real, can also be documented. The same is true of the hints of Richelieu's romantic interest in the queen and even of such a detail as Buckingham's order to close the English ports while the duplicate studs are being made (Chapter XXI).[1]

Besides the obviously historical figures in the novel—Louis XIII, Anne d'Autriche, Richelieu, and Buckingham—the large majority of other characters too have counterparts in history. D'Artagnan, Athos, Porthos, and Aramis were all real people. Milady, Constance Bonacieux, and de Wardes have all been identified, or at least plausibly associated, with known individuals. A host of characters mentioned in passing bear historical names. Even John Felton, Milady's young English "jailer," was in fact, as in the book, the assassin of the Duke of Buckingham. But in *Les Trois Mousquetaires* Dumas was writing a novel, not history. If a knowledge of history is unnecessary in order to enjoy it—indeed, too thorough a knowledge may be a distraction—a glance at the principal changes Dumas made and his probable reasons for them can most effectively illuminate his methods and his conception of the historical romance.

In a brief preface Dumas introduces the tale he is about to begin as a first publication of the manuscript memoirs of the comte de la Fère. Both manuscript and author are, of course, completely imaginary; Dumas is simply playing a conventional little game with his readers. In the same preface, however, he does indirectly acknowledge the real principal source of his story: the *Mémoires de Monsieur d'Artagnan*. Dumas was apparently unaware that the memoirs of d'Artagnan, while not as imaginary as those of his supposed count, were themselves spurious—the work of Gatien Courtilz de Sandras, published about thirty years after the real d'Artagnan's death. Their authenticity obviously matters less than Dumas's acceptance of them. Their importance lies in the extent to which they stimulated his imagination and gave him starting point and substance for his novel.

From these pseudomemoirs Dumas drew the character of d'Artagnan and the names of Athos, Porthos, and Aramis (friends in Dumas's novel, in Courtilz they are brothers and much less prominent figures). The opening episodes—d'Artagnan's departure from home, the encounter at Meung (including the characters of Rochefort and Milady), d'Artagnan's settling in Paris, his meeting with M. de Tréville and his three future friends, his first duels and the fight with Richelieu's guards, the characters (but not the names) of M. and Mme Bonacieux—also come from Courtilz, though incidents and characters all undergo development at Dumas's hands. Much of this development comes from Dumas's rich imagination and love of concrete detail; much comes also from his knowledge of the period absorbed from his extensive reading of other—authentic—memoirs. But the direction that the development takes is to a large degree determined by one significant change that Dumas made in his hero: he made him ten years older than he was in history.

Thus lifted from his proper historical context and placed in another one, d'Artagnan becomes a fictional creation. The events in which this fictional d'Artagnan participates were real ones, as he was a real person, but because his role in them is an imagined one both characters and events now partake of a new reality, that of the novel. It is in terms of this new reality and its exigencies that d'Artagnan develops and acts. Dumas takes such liberties as he needs to with fact; where facts are unavailable or unusable he has a framework for invention.

Pure invention plays a greater part in the creation of Athos, Porthos, and Aramis simply because Dumas had less to work with. Less was known of their historical models and their role in the pseudomemoirs is more episodic than the one Dumas chose to give them. At the same time, as in the case of d'Artagnan, Dumas strengthens the sense of their historical validity by having them perform, whenever possible, deeds that though not performed by them were nonetheless really executed by someone.

The character of Milady reveals further aspects of Dumasian inventiveness. Again Dumas starts with a character he found in the *Mémoires de M. d'Artagnan.* As enigmatic and mysterious there as. in *Les Trois Mousquetaires,* she is much less than the pervasive nemesis of d'Artagnan and his companions that she becomes in Dumas's hands. He develops her as a character and expands her role by both appropriation and invention. He borrows from history, giving her in the affair of the diamond studs the role that had actually been played by a former mistress of Buckingham, Lady Carlisle.[2] He borrows from another book of spurious memoirs attributed to Courtilz de Sandras the important episode in which d'Artagnan, replacing de Wardes in Milady's chamber for a night, discovers the fleur-de-lis branded on her shoulder.[3] And he enriches her characterization from his own imagination by such devices as the past he attributes to her—former *galérienne* and repudiated wife of Athos—and by having her, in order to accomplish both her escape and her mission, motivate John Felton to kill Buckingham. Milady's foil in the novel, the winsome Constance Bonacieux, is a similar combination of characters drawn from Courtilz, from history (Mmes de Vernet and du Fargis of the *suite* of Anne of Austria[4]), and Dumas's imagination.

Only a word needs to be said about Louis XIII, Anne d'Autriche, Richelieu, and Buckingham. Though none of them—least of all in the 1620's—would have had contact with d'Artagnan, each of them otherwise plays substantially his authentic role. In his depiction of them Dumas follows contemporary sources faithfully, simplifying and dramatizing more than he changes. If he invents dialogue for them and puts them in imaginary situations with more-or-less fictitious characters, he always does so with skill and verisimilitude. For these reasons the characterizations remain, in their broad lines, consistent with history. Such consistency also fits Dumas's aims as a novelist. It was manifestly because he wanted to evoke these particular personages and their period that he transported his musketeer heroes back in time. His task then was to portray them and their drama as convincingly as he could.

We have noted that the action of *Les Trois Mousquetaires,* like its characters, is drawn substantially from historical sources, or at least from what Dumas believed to be such. As he did with characters, Dumas adapts and alters events; his version of the siege of La Rochelle is typical of his procedure.

Since the siege in reality was long, he compresses the action. Selecting key episodes to develop, he skips over others and over long periods of time in between, while still observing chronological sequence. He makes the historical siege more integral to the action by making it a confrontation between his characters as well as a military action directed by Richelieu against a Protestant stronghold:

> Richelieu, as everyone knows, had been in love with the queen. . . .
> For Richelieu, then, it was a question not only of ridding France of an enemy but of avenging himself on a rival. . . .
> Richelieu knew that in fighting England he was fighting Buckingham . . . that in humiliating England in the eyes of Europe he was humiliating Buckingham in the eyes of the queen.
> For his part, Buckingham, while defending the honor of England, was moved by concerns exactly comparable to those of the cardinal; Buckingham also was pursuing a personal vengeance. . . .
> Consequently the true stake in this match, engaged in by the two most powerful kingdoms at the whim of two men in love, was a simple glance from Anne of Austria.
>
> (Chapter XLI, "Le Siège de La Rochelle")

Dumas obviously knew his public well enough to recognize that passion would have broader appeal than politics. But however far-fetched and melodramatic this interpretation of the issues at stake at La Rochelle may be, it could be admitted without necessarily doing violence to recorded events. In the case of the musketeers Dumas handled matters somewhat differently. Though d'Artagnan, Athos, Porthos, and Aramis did not participate in the siege, the known presence there of the King's Musketeers lends plausibility to their activities. Yet Dumas does not hesitate to introduce a completely fictional incident—the taking of the Bastion Saint-Gervais—to give them the kind of adventure he wants them to have just then and to provide a transition he deems necessary between other episodes.

In and around such inventions, as well as in the web of real events, Dumas incorporates countless little touches—details of manners and dress, passing incidents and allusions, familiar or unusual names—which all contribute concretely to the "feel" of the period. When a real name or a genuine incident can be used to heighten the sense of historical authenticity, Dumas rarely fails to do so, be it a signature on an order or a ballet for Louis XIII to dance.

But Dumas can and does slip on occasion. His mistakes are usually inadvertent, due sometimes to ignorance, more often to forgetfulness, distraction, or simply the tremendous speed at which he wrote and his notoriously careless proofreading. Wrong and inconsistent spelling abounds in his novels, especially in the case of foreign names. His classic and most frequently cited historical error occurs in the d'Artagnan trilogy: he several times uses house numbers, which were not introduced in Paris until 150 years after the era in which he set these novels. More than once, too, he innocently refers to streets by their nineteenth century names rather than by those they bore two centuries earlier. He mislocates the house of M. de Tréville in Paris and fails to catch a number of anachronisms that stem from moving his hero's early adventures a decade back. He assigns a different date to Milady's safe-conduct pass from Richelieu each of the three times he quotes it, though this may be a discreet attempt at masking a potentially more obvious error in chronology. Such slips, though numerous, are rarely significant and they commonly escape all but the most attentive reader. They certainly do not constitute a real deformation of history—least of all by a writer who, even in his most serious moments, could lay no claim to being either a precise or a scientific historian.

But if Dumas was never a scientific historian, he was first, last, and always a dramatist. Both in their conception and their execution his novels, no less surely than his plays, reveal his essentially dramatic vision of the world. This vision is reflected in Dumas's incomparable sense of situation, his instinctive reduction of complex or abstract issues to concrete human conflicts, his awareness of the roles—often multiple—that individuals play in their constantly varying confrontations. It is expressed through all the devices, if not all the dimensions, of drama, but most tellingly in the primary importance he attaches to action and episode as opposed to narrative and description.

In *Les Trois Mousquetaires* we are plunged immediately into the action: "The first Monday of April, 1625, the town of Meung, where the author of the *Roman de la Rose* was born, seemed to be in the throes of as total a revolution as if the Huguenots had come to make of it a second La Rochelle." In this setting—evoked in terms of movement and mood, not physical description—Dumas's "Don Quixote at eighteen," riding his yellow *bidet de Béarn*, makes his entrance. When the reader needs to know what brings him there a flashback permits the exposition to be accomplished by equally concrete, dramatic means, and the reader is quickly transported again into the midst of the crowd watching d'Artagnan's arrival. A moment later the insult occurs, d'Artagnan's antagonists are introduced, and the plot is engaged in a flurry of verbal exchanges and swordplay. Four short paragraphs at the end of the chapter carry d'Artagnan from Meung to Paris, establish him there, and leave him ready to call on M. de Tréville. In contrast with the full development of the events at Meung, the very conciseness of these paragraphs emphasizes Dumas's approach to his story as a series of episodes connected only by as much narrative transition as is absolutely necessary. The prologue over, the curtain is now ready to rise on Act I.

Dominance of dialogue and action, thus apparent from the opening pages, is a constant in *Les Trois Mousquetaires* as it is in virtually all of Dumas's novels. There is narration, of course, and explanation, wherever they are essential (for example, in the passage cited from Chapter XLI). Dumas never hesitates to intervene and address the reader directly. Like contemporaries such as Balzac and Stendhal, Dumas sees no reason to pretend that it is not he, after all, who is telling the story. But chapter after chapter filled with rapid dialogue speeds the tale along and lets the characters act it out. The sense of speed is underscored by the terseness of the narration, the series of short paragraphs—often single sentences—that ordinarily comprise it. It is often observed that Dumas's paragraphing and extended dialogues reflect his desire to capitalize on being paid by the line of printed text. This may be true, and seems especially so in some of the more sprawling novels, but the stylistic effect remains. It too often calls to mind the crackling dialogue and rush of events in the plays to be entirely accidental. And the devices of melodrama—surprise, coincidence, terror—which are exploited here as in the plays are all dependent on the maintenance of pace, a fact of which Dumas would be the last to be unaware.

Les Trois Mousquetaires is built around three principal historical actions—the queen's diamonds, the siege of La Rochelle, and the assassination of Buckingham—which are like the acts in a drama on a grand scale. Against and within this framework Dumas's characters work out their destinies. This underlying structural simplicity in a plot rich in surface complications and unexpected twists further reminds us that Dumas was also a playwright. Characters are painted in broad strokes and elaborated cumulatively rather than analytically, through their deeds and words rather than reflection about them. Suspense and comic relief are manipulated with skill and faultless timing—witness the juxtaposition of Porthos's amusing courtship of Mme Coquenard and d'Artagnan's melodramatic "wooing" of Milady, or d'Artagnan's return home wearing the clothes of Milady's maid after the violent scene in her chamber and his hairbreadth escape. Perhaps the most masterly—and in a sense most subtly theatrical—episode in the book is the taking of the Bastion Saint-Gervais, with its superb mixture of high comedy and genuine suspense, real heroism and burlesque. And if other proof is needed of the justness of the term *"roman-drame"* ("novel-drama") that Sigaux applies to Dumas's historical romances,[5] one need look no farther than the chapter endings. Designed to whet the appetite of the *feuilleton* reader for the next installment, they slice through the book like so many breathtaking "curtains," compelling the reader to turn the page and let the next act commence.

We have dealt at some length with Dumas's treatment of history in *Les Trois Mousquetaires* and with the form of that novel because, in a general way, the same observations can be made about all his historical novels. As in his plays, Dumas used tried and true methods in his novels as long as they worked. Technical innovations held little interest for him as such; style was something he admired in other writers but was too busy to concern himself with in his own writing beyond saying what he wanted to say simply, directly, and entertainingly.

But, having examined his methods, we have still said little about Dumas's real achievement in *Les Trois Mousquetaires*. Whatever liberties and mistakes may be ascribed to him, in this novel he has produced a convincing illusion of historical reality, bringing a remote period to life with exceptional immediacy and concreteness. He has told a rich and absorbing tale of adventure with matchless verve, humor, and inventiveness. And he has created memorable characters, at once types and artfully individualized, simple but always believable. To a degree he did all these things in his plays also, but even his greatest theatrical triumphs neither penetrated far beyond the borders of France nor outlived his century. The enduring international popularity of *Les Trois Mousquetaires* is ample demonstration that here Dumas has transcended limits of country and time to attain universality.

Universality in characters: Milady—evil personified, the classic *femme fatale;* Athos, Porthos, Aramis—together symbols of daring and fraternal loyalty; separately noble, pompous and devious, mysterious, engaging and secretive; d'Artagnan—the most complex and greatest creation of them all—archetypal Gascon, rash yet prudent, courageous and sentimental, idealistic yet shrewdly ambitious. Like these characters, a gallery of others, great and small, live both in and beyond the pages of history and romance.

Universality in vision: D'Artagnan arriving in Meung is every cowboy arriving, ready for adventure, in a little western town,[6] as he is also every young hero of a *Bildungsroman* embarking on his education in the ways of the world. Conflicts assume the dimensions of struggles between right and wrong, good and evil, while conversely nations go to war because their leaders, for all their rank and power, are no less subject to the very human failings of jealousy and vengefulness.

Universality in theme: The idealism of youth, the thirst for glory, the thrill of worlds to conquer and the urgency of noble causes to defend, readiness to risk all for the sake of friendship or love—such are the themes and values embodied in the world of d'Artagnan and the musketeers as conceived by Dumas. But if they reflect first of all his own Romantic outlook, they also speak to a deeper Romanticism, inherent perhaps in human nature, that knows no limits of time or place. In this appeal to universal feelings and strivings lies the secret of the fascination of this perennially youthful work.

II   Vingt Ans après

Against a background of civil strife in France and England, d'Artagnan and his comrades return to action *Twenty Years After.* Richelieu and Louis XIII are dead. Anne d'Autriche and Cardinal Mazarin now govern in the name of the ten-year-old Louis XIV. Paris is agitated and feelings are running high against the prime minister as the first Fronde breaks out in 1648. "France weakened, the king's authority unrecognized, the nobles again strong and rebellious, the enemy again at the doorstep—everything bore witness that Richelieu was no longer there" (Chapter I).

D'Artagnan is still there, still a lieutenant in the King's Musketeers. But as times have changed d'Artagnan has changed with them. Forty years old, with graying hair, he has lost his youthful enthusiasm and chafes at the routine and anonymity that now characterize his life. He is discouraged by his loneliness, the indifference of the queen, and the irregularity with which he is paid, and wistfully recalls the excitement and challenge of life with his friends, in the days of Richelieu, now fondly remembered as the "great" cardinal. Eager to revive his zest for life and to devote himself to a cause—as well as, perhaps, to earn a promotion— d'Artagnan accepts Mazarin's proposal that he seek out his old comrades-at-arms and persuade them to join in active service of the prime minister. He learns quickly that Aramis and Athos are partisan to the Fronde; only Porthos is willing to join him.

But if, as d'Artagnan boasted, the two of them were worth twelve ordinary men, they were not the equal of the famous four, as their first mission proved. Pursuing the duc de Beaufort after his escape from prison in Vincennes they fail to capture him. More distressing to them even than this failure is the discovery that their opponents in the encounter with the duke's men turn out to be Athos and Aramis. A nocturnal meeting in the Place Royale reconciles the four and they reaffirm mutual personal loyalty irrespective of political commitments.

While Athos and Aramis leave for England with Lord de Winter to go to the aid of the beleaguered king, Charles I, d'Artagnan and Porthos remain in a Paris more and more seething with resentment of Mazarin, his policies, and his influence over the queen. Riots occur and there are threats of revolution. When Anne d'Autriche decides to flee with the king and Mazarin to Saint-Germain,[7] d'Artagnan and Porthos successfully engineer the escape; they are then immediately dispatched to England to deliver a letter from Mazarin to Oliver Cromwell. Not knowing that Athos and Aramis are in England also, d'Artagnan and Porthos are again surprised to encounter them in battle, again in the opposing camp. This time, however, in the clash between the forces of Cromwell and those of Charles I that ends with the capture of the king, it is d'Artagnan and Porthos who are the nominal victors over their former comrades and who "capture" them in order to help them ultimately to escape. Since their mission for Mazarin is now accomplished, d'Artagnan and Porthos decide to join forces with Athos and Aramis and try to liberate the captive Charles I.

After their efforts fail and the king is executed the four friends return to France, going to Paris separately for safety. Mazarin's agents intercept d'Artagnan and Porthos en route and arrest them; Athos is arrested in turn when he goes to the queen and asks to know the whereabouts of his missing comrades. Imprisoned near each other in Saint-Germain, they contrive not only to escape but to abduct Mazarin at the same time, taking him to Porthos' castle of Pierrefonds. There they hold him prisoner until he accedes to the demands of the leaders of the Fronde and signs their proposed treaty (which Aramis has conveniently in his pocket). In exchange for Mazarin's release the queen also signs the treaty. Before the court returns to Paris, however, d'Artagnan eloquently persuades the queen to make Porthos a baron and him, at long last, captain of the Musketeers.

Two new characters appear in secondary but important roles in *Vingt Ans après*: Mordaunt (John Francis de Winter), the son of Milady; and Raoul de Bragelonne, the son of Athos and the Duchesse de Chevreuse. Mordaunt figures principally in the English episodes, seeking vengeance on the musketeers for the death of his mother and himself coming to a horrifying end. The vicomte de Bragelonne, who knows Athos only as his guardian, is shown in his devotion to the seven-year-old Louise de La Vallière, foreshadowing the love story in the sequel which bears his name. At the end of this novel Athos entrusts him to the care of d'Artagnan as he returns to his home in Touraine and Raoul embarks on a military career.

Among the first things to strike the reader of *Vingt Ans après* are not only the links but the parallels between this novel and its predecessor. *Les Trois Mousquetaires* was constructed around three major historical occurrences. *Vingt Ans après* is built around two— the first Fronde in Paris and the Revolution in England—and, as in the earlier work, the action is divided between those two countries, with brief excursions into the Ile-de-France, Picardy, and Flanders. The treatment and use of history are comparable, as is the manner of interweaving fact and fiction. The narration sparkles with humor and crackles with suspense, the characters reveal themselves

primarily through dialogue and action. D'Artagnan and the
musketeers are again at cross-purposes with a cardinal–prime
minister whom they variously serve and try to outguess. Yet from
the very first page differences between the two books emerge as
more profound than the resemblances.

The title of the novel prepares the reader for change, and it is the
changes that have occurred in familiar characters and familiar places
that form the substance of the opening section. Chapter I, "The
Ghost of Richelieu," deliberately begins with an image that could
have come from the earlier book, then sets the stage for new action
by contrasting first the character, methods, and reputation of the
new cardinal with those of Richelieu, then the appearance and
atmosphere of Paris in January, 1648, with the city as it had been
twenty years before. Succeeding chapters bring together d'Artagnan
and the comte de Rochefort, his erstwhile "man from Meung," now
no longer his enemy; introduce Anne d'Autriche at forty-six; and
affectionately delineate the man d'Artagnan has become at forty.
Leaving Paris with d'Artagnan the reader journeys to Noisy-le-Sec
to find Aramis, now the abbé d'Herblay and deeply involved in
political intrigue; to Pierrefonds near Dumas's native Villers-
Cotterêts to find Porthos, how a widowed and wealthy country
gentleman; and to the château of Bragelonne near Blois where
Athos, under his true name of the comte de la Fère, is devoting his
life to rearing his son.

Thus stressing the changes that have occurred, Dumas
underscores the separateness of the musketeers' present lives, a
separateness intensified by the discovery of their opposing
allegiances. Their former total mutual trust is now replaced by
doubt and suspicion, their uncertainties paralleling those of the
times, the deviousness of Mazarin, and the division within societies
in both France and England. Unlike the warring factions in those
two countries the four comrades are able to achieve reconciliation
and the security of knowing they will not betray each other; yet
through much of the book, like the peoples of France and England,
they are divided by conflicting political loyalties and duties and their
shared causes are temporary. They are no longer invincible, apart or
together. Their greatest joint effort—the attempt to save Charles
I—is a lost cause from the start, and more often than not they are
working against each other. If together they overcome Mordaunt
and defeat Mazarin's scheming, their triumphs do not bind them

together for long and they are soon second-guessing each other again. D'Artagnan especially relies constantly on his knowledge of his friends' characters, as well as on his native astuteness, to anticipate their behavior and guarantee the results he wants. At the end it seems not only inevitable but natural that they should part once more and return to their separate lives.

But change is not limited to the characters and their relationships; it is found also in the form and manner of the book. Longer than *Les Trois Mousquetaires, Vingt Ans après* is also much more episodic in structure and frequently more leisurely in the telling. If there seems to be less verve at times—in keeping, intentionally or not, with the middle-aged status of the heroes—there is more deliberate humor in it and more extended exploration of characters' emotions and opinions. Finally, there are differences in the relationship between the central figures and the key actions in the novel.

The structure is more episodic because the two main actions are fundamentally unrelated and involve different people as well as locales. Further, because events are frequently concurrent Dumas is, more often than in *Les Trois Mousquetaires*, forced to interrupt the narrative and move back and forth in time and space. More importantly, though, the historical basis of this novel is not reducible to the kind of tightly woven plot found in the earlier romance. The events of the first Fronde can in no way be forced into a complex but cohesive narrative like the story of the queen's diamonds because the Fronde was a different kind of historical happening. The episodes are widely divergent and often involve completely different actors; related but not continuous, they are like a series of tapestries rather than the interlocked links of a chain. The duc de Beaufort, for example, makes a dramatic escape from the château of Vincennes and then, except for an occasional allusion, disappears from the novel. The next major episode of the Fronde that Dumas recounts is the imprisonment and release of Broussel. This, of course, bears a relationship to the escape of the duc de Beaufort, but on the political level, not on that of drama or plot. The scenes with Henrietta Maria in Paris offer considerable historic— even dramatic—interest in themselves and provide a kind of link between the French and English portions of the book, but they do not significantly advance the plot beyond giving a pretext for Athos and Aramis to go to England and they remain memorable chiefly in isolation. The presence of Mordaunt and Raoul de Bragelonne similarly provides useful links, in one case with the past, in the other with the future; but again, whatever their intrinsic interest, the episodes in which they figure are largely extraneous to the central concerns of the book and consequently heighten rather than diminish the feeling of discontinuity.

Dumas was obviously aware of the problem, however, and managed to impose a valid unity on his novel despite the difficulties inherent in his chosen subject. Unity is achieved principally through d'Artagnan, who remains in center stage virtually from start to finish. Dumas also makes effective use of parallel, contrast, and symmetry in structure. Through the entire first half of this book there hovers an uneasy concern about the legitimacy of the musketeers' vengeance on Milady. D'Artagnan's doubts are echoed by those of Athos, and their recurrent sense of guilt is finally exorcised only at the death of Mordaunt. Mordaunt and Raoul are reincarnations of the old opposing forces; irony colors the symmetry of their identities—offspring of Athos' repudiated wife and of Athos himself—and the contrast between their characters and roles. In *Les Trois Mousquetaires* Milady was responsible for Athos' moroseness and drinking; while Raoul in this novel has given Athos the incentive to triumph over his weakness, it is Mordaunt, Milady's son, who enables him finally to lay her ghost to rest. Without reference to events in *Les Trois Mousquetaires* there is still a satisfying symmetry within *Vingt Ans après* that also works toward unity; the two *Te Deums*, the first heralding the victory at Lens, the second the return of the king to Paris—another kind of victory; the ruse of Mazarin reflected in the cunning employed by the musketeers both for and against him; and the cardinal's arrest of the musketeers followed by their abduction of him.

In both of these first two novels of the d'Artagnan trilogy Dumas has his protagonists figure in major historical events in which their real counterparts did not participate at all. There is a significant difference between the books, however, in the nature of their participation. In *Vingt Ans apres* the roles of the four comrades are essentially passive. Despite their almost constant presence in the narrative and their considerable activity, they are for the most part not truly instrumental in bringing about or affecting the outcome of the principal events. Only in the flight of the court from Paris and in the completely fictitious abduction of Mazarin do they play a decisive role and engage in the kind of exploits that fill the pages of

Les Trois Mousquetaires. This is partly a result of the choice of events: the duc de Beaufort, for example, could not have been recaptured, nor could Charles I have escaped execution. But it is also a function of the nature of the events themselves, those characteristics that give the book its episodic structure. The roles of the musketeers must be secondary for the sake of history, but for every other reason they must be given first importance. Dumas involves them in the historical action with great ingenuity but he cannot make them integral to it as he did in *Les Trois Mousquetaires*.

Perhaps at least partly because of this distance between his characters and the historical background of the novel, but surely to a considerable degree because Dumas is as interested in d'Artagnan and his friends as he knows his readers to be, there is more characterization through description in *Vingt Ans après* than in its predecessor—indeed there is more emphasis on characterization as such. Dumas still uses his familiar dramatic devices, however, and so artfully that the reader is almost startled, for example, to realize that nothing really happens in the first eighteen chapters. Up to that point d'Artagnan is simply discovering the past and present of his former comrades-at-arms and being revealed anew to the reader himself. This leisurely opening, along with other carefully controlled variations in pace, contributes to a general spaciousness and a degree of mellowness that typify the entire book and reflect the present ages of the characters, just as their vitality and brashness paralleled the fast-moving action in the earlier book. Dumas has further both aged and developed his characters with many well-chosen touches that still preserve the known personal traits, be they the slyness and vanity of Aramis (who tries to subtract five years from his real age), the pomposity and loyalty of Porthos, the nobility of Athos or the Gascon shrewdness of d'Artagnan. The reader, in the end, can only be delighted to find his friends still so much themselves, and if *Vingt Ans après* taken as a whole does not quite equal *Les Trois Mousquetaires*, it is nonetheless a worthy successor.

III Le Vicomte de Bragelonne

Markedly greater differences separate *The Viscount of Bragelonne* from the earlier novels in the d'Artagnan trilogy than had separated those two works from each other. It is twice the length of *Les Trois Mousquetaires* and *Vingt Ans après* together—

some 1800–2000 pages—and its structure is more complicated than either of theirs. For both of these reasons it becomes a different kind of novel, though no less essential a part of the trilogy.

The length and complexity of *Le Vicomte de Bragelonne* are related to the period of time and the range of events it encompasses. Where *Les Trois Mousquetaires* and *Vingt Ans après* each covered a period of two to three years, *Le Vicomte de Bragelonne* embraces thirteen—from the journey of Louis XIV to meet his Spanish bride in May, 1660, to the death of d'Artagnan in June, 1673. While each of the earlier novels concentrates on two or three major events around which the plot is developed, this one relates four connected but distinct stories—so distinct that they have on occasion been adapted for separate publication. The first two introduced concern the restoration of Charles II of England and the love affair of Louis XIV and Louise de La Vallière; the other two recount the fall of Fouquet and the famous tale of the Man in the Iron Mask. The wealth of incident is equalled by the size of the cast of characters, which includes even Molière and La Fontaine in the episode of Fouquet and his unlucky fête at Vaux-le-Vicomte.

But the differences go beyond length and intricacy of plot. In *Vingt Ans après* d'Artagnan, Athos, Porthos, and Aramis played more passive roles than they had in *Les Trois Mousquetaires*, but they—especially d'Artagnan—remained in the foreground. In *Le Vicomte de Bragelonne* their roles are not only less influential but more episodic; the historical panorama now dominates, with the result that the novel becomes not a tightly plotted drama but a sweeping pageant, the chronicle of a decade with no single hero or group of heroes, no single core of action. The reader who approaches this book expecting another *Trois Mousquetaires*, or simply another novel about d'Artagnan and his companions, risks disappointment, for there are long stretches in which none of them appears and the plot seems at times to go in several directions at once. Yet the book is not without its attractions and its devotees; "no part of the world has ever seemed to me so charming as these pages, and not even my friends are quite so real, perhaps quite so dear, as d'Artagnan," wrote Robert Louis Stevenson.[8] And he continues:

What other novel has such epic variety and nobility of incident? often, if you will, impossible; often of the order of an Arabian story; and yet all based in human nature. For if you come to that, what novel has more human nature? not studied with the microscope, but seen largely, in plain daylight, with the natural eye? What novel has more good sense, and gaiety, and wit, and unflagging, admirable literary skill? Good souls, I suppose, must sometimes read it in the blackguard travesty of a translation. But there is no style so untranslatable; light as a whipped trifle, strong as silk; wordy like a village tale; pat like a general's despatch; with every fault, yet never tedious; with no merit, yet inimitably right.[9]

Stevenson's enthusiasm does not blind him to the book's flaws, especially to its most glaring weakness: the title character. Raoul de Bragelonne remains an impossibly unreal stick, undeveloped in any significant way from *Vingt Ans après*, not only unconvincing but ultimately tiresome. Fortunately, despite giving his name to the book, like the musketeers he appears only at intervals. Louise de La Vallière, though not a totally successful creation either, manages to stir more interest and sympathy in the reader. Far more impressive than either of these characterizations is that of the young Louis XIV during the first dozen years of his personal reign: vain, sensuous, pampered; jealous, self-centered, yet unmistakably regal as he tests his authority and moves toward being the monarch he has envisioned. A profusion of other portraits—some only sketched, others elaborated at length, most of them based directly on contemporary memoirs—surround the central figures and illuminate this pageant of history with colors both vivid and authentic. But for the reader who has come to this book by way of its two predecessors the center of interest remains—inevitably— d'Artagnan and, next to him, Athos, Porthos, and Aramis.

The historical Athos and Porthos had died before the events related in *Vingt Ans après* occurred and Aramis, though perhaps still alive in the 1660's, was never either bishop of Vannes or general of the Jesuits as Dumas makes him. Their roles in this novel, then, are obviously imaginary. Dumas depicts the trio again as he did before, with only a modicum of exaggeration in their familiar characteristics. Athos, aristocratic and devoted to noble causes, collaborates with d'Artagnan to help bring about the restoration of Charles II. Porthos loyally and a bit stupidly abets the plotting of Aramis, then dies heroically after displaying the physical prowess of a dozen men. Aramis, less lovable than ever, schemes and connives with Fouquet against Louis XIV in the fortification of Belle-Isle and in the plot to place the mysterious prisoner in the iron mask on Louis's throne. Pardoned by the king through d'Artagnan's efforts, of the four only he is still alive when the novel reaches its end.

Unlike his comrades, d'Artagnan not only appears in an imagined role but actually performs some of the actions of his historical model. The real d'Artagnan too arrested Fouquet and guarded him during part of his long imprisonment; like Dumas's hero he died on the field of battle fighting the Dutch, though without winning the baton of a marshal of France. Yet the historical veracity of d'Artagnan's deeds here is no longer important, for he has by this novel achieved so complete an identity in the world of fiction that he lives independently. A. C. Bell observed[10] that Dumas has accomplished the feat of creating a character so intensely real that his slightest act or gesture now is of consuming interest to the reader. Few would dispute this remark after noting the effect of every reappearance of d'Artagnan in this long narrative. However absorbing Dumas's evocations of the splendors, intrigues, and adventures of seventeenth century court life in France may be, never do they attain alone the vitality and fascination or the immediacy they assume whenever d'Artagnan is involved. To understand this power of Dumas's hero we turn again to Stevenson's appreciation:

D'Artagnan has mellowed into a man so witty, rough, kind, and upright, that he takes the heart by storm. There is nothing of the copy-book about his virtues, nothing of the drawing-room in his fine, natural civility; he will sail near the wind; he is no district visitor—no Wesley or Robespierre; his conscience is void of all refinement whether for good or evil; but the whole man rings true like a good sovereign.[11]

In this capacity for "taking the heart by storm," in this "ringing true," we find the real measure and quality not only of d'Artagnan but of the three novels in which he figures. Unevenness, weaknesses, errors, faults—all these mean little. It is their positive virtues, the universality of their appeal, and above all their unforgettable hero that have kept these books alive for more than a century and that give every sign of continuing to enchant generations ahead.

CHAPTER 6

The Valois Cycle

WITH his "Valois Cycle," written between 1845 and 1848, Dumas returns to the historical period that furnished his first theatrical triumph nearly twenty years before—the bloody era of the religious wars and the reigns of the last two kings of the Valois line, Charles IX and Henri III, sons of Henri II and Catherine de Médicis. The cycle contains three novels: *La Reine Margot (Marguerite de Valois), La Dame de Monsoreau (The Lady of Monsoreau,* titled *Chicot the Jester* in some English versions), and *Les Quarante-Cinq (The Forty-Five* or *Forty-Five Guardsmen).* The ending of *Les Quarante-Cinq* makes it quite evident that Dumas had contemplated a fourth novel to complete the series, but none was actually started.[1]

The three works we have, each focussing on a space of one or two years, together span the period from August, 1572, to June, 1586. In them Dumas treats historical fact in characteristic fashion—compressing time, shifting dates, and combining events as he needs to, though without altering the period in which his leading characters move as he had done in *Les Trois Mousquetaires.* But if the books in this series offer no new insights on the question of Dumas and history, as novels they rank among his strongest achievements. Their literary qualities are representative of those found in all his most admired works and their best pages are equal to his best anywhere. It is primarily from the standpoint of Dumas's art, then, that we shall examine them.

I La Reine Margot

The opening chapters of *La Reine Margot* are a superb example of controlled suspense and skillfully dramatized exposition. Beginning, as he so commonly does, with a precise statement of the date—Monday, 18 August 1572—Dumas plunges into a lively evocation of

the wedding festivities of Henri de Navarre and Marguerite de
Valois, depicting simultaneously the surface gaiety and the
underlying tensions in this alliance between a Protestant prince and
a Catholic princess, neither of whom has any interest other than
political in the marriage. During the fête Marguerite and her lover,
the duc de Guise, make a rendezvous for that night, while Henri de
Navarre much less discreetly arranges to spend his wedding night
with Charlotte de Sauve,[2] lady-in-waiting to Catherine de Médicis.
Later Henri and Marguerite make a pact of mutual "political"
loyalty, with no questions to be asked on the personal level. Having
overheard this agreement—with Marguerite's knowledge—Guise
uses it as a pretext to break with his mistress.

Other principal actors in the drama are introduced in rapid
succession. By shrewd choice of the incidents he uses to do this and
by skillful bridging of the lapses of time between them, Dumas
shapes the events from the royal wedding to the St. Bartholomew's
Day massacre into one smooth crescendo of suspense. First King
Charles IX is shown affectionately conversing with Admiral Coligny,
chief of the Huguenots; then, in an ominous interview between the
king and Maurevel, a paid assassin, Charles IX orders the death of
the man for whom he has just professed friendship. Leaving the
Louvre in Chapter IV, the narrative passes on to the two young
protagonists of the novel, the Provençal comte Hyacinthe Lérac de
La Mole and the Piémontais Marc-Annibal de Coconnas as they
meet before an inn in the rue de l'Arbre-Sec early in the evening of
August 24th. Their good-natured provincial bragging and instinctive
mutual sympathy contrast sharply with the ambivalent tone of the
preceding episodes: but as the reader follows them to the Louvre,
where La Mole seeks the Protestant Henri de Navarre and
Coconnas the Catholic duc de Guise, complications are foreseen for
them. One final scene in the Louvre, which introduces Catherine
de Médicis with Charles IX, completes the exposition.

With the stage thus set, the actors in place, and the springs of
action wound tight, the tocsin sounds from the church of Saint-
Germain-l'Auxerrois and the bloody drama of the *Saint-Barthélemy*
is unleashed. Following first La Mole, then Coconnas, Dumas leads
the reader through the carnage in the streets, into the Louvre and
out, to the Hôtel de Guise in the Marais, to the home of Coligny at
the moment of the admiral's murder. Like La Mole and Coconnas
the reader is swept along in spite of himself. The horror and the

confusion of events is vividly conveyed, while the device of a focal
character prevents total disorientation of the reader and lends a
remarkable sense of direct involvement. Clarity and swiftness of
narration are further aided by the previous identification of almost
all the characters so that their presence and roles require no
explanatory interruptions.

A sudden contrast is provided in Chapter X by a shift of the action
from the din of the streets to the hushed interior of the Louvre. In
Marguerite's room she and her lady-in-waiting Gillonne are tending
the wounded La Mole, who has sought refuge there, when the
distraught and terrified Charlotte de Sauve enters, looking for
Henri de Navarre. Meanwhile, in the king's apartments, Henri and
Charles IX confront each other, individual symbols of the forces
clashing outside. Catherine de Médicis hovers near and, at the
climax of the quarrel, when the frenzied Charles IX has just
threatened the life of Henri unless he abjures his Protestant faith,
Marguerite enters and affirms, before her mother and brother, her
loyalty to her husband.

This chapter demonstrates with exceptional concreteness how
Dumas's sense of drama informs his novels, determining both
substance and development. The memoirs of the historical
Marguerite de Valois contain the story of a young wounded
Huguenot who sought—and received—protection in her chambers
during the massacre. The anecdote was too rich in humanity and
dramatic irony for Dumas to resist, but the theatrical craftsman was
reluctant to introduce a new character with no further role to play.
By identifying the protagonist of his novel with the hero of this
episode Dumas simultaneously retained a colorful and historically
valid incident, heightened its dramatic value, and laid a plausible
groundwork for the liaison between Marguerite and La Mole that
develops in subsequent chapters.

The action in this chapter unfolds through a series of entrances
and confrontations of mounting intensity. La Mole and Charlotte de
Sauve arrive successively in Marguerite's room; first Henri, then
Catherine de Médicis, finally Marguerite enter the king's
apartment. Marguerite confronts first a stranger in desperate need,
then her husband's mistress. The confrontation of the two kings is
followed by the alliance of Catherine and Charles against Henri,
then by another shift of forces as Marguerite takes her stand beside
her husband. By setting these personal and political conflicts against

the background of the bloody battle still raging in the streets in the name of religion, Dumas enlarges the implications and the drama of both.

Other chapters and episodes are shaped with comparable care to achieve contrast, variety, and suspense. Chapter XXXIV illustrates Dumas's deft handling of simultaneous actions. It recounts an ambush planned by Catherine de Médicis intended to culminate in the murder of Henri de Navarre by Maurevel. The reader has been informed of Catherine's plot but is also aware, as she is not, that Henri has secretly absented himself from the palace, leaving his room occupied by his young Protestant ally De Mouy, sworn enemy of Maurevel.

Dumas opens the chapter with Catherine in her apartments, quietly listening as Charlotte de Sauve reads to her. Impassive in her confidence that she knows what is happening, Catherine keeps her personal guard and Charlotte in the room as sounds of fighting echo from Henri's apartment, despite the guard's curiosity and Charlotte's ill-concealed fears for her lover. The sounds cease and the reading continues when, unexpectedly, new and more violent noises are heard, accompanied this time by heavy footsteps and gunshots. Even Catherine is startled by this, but her attendants are still held back as she announces that she, herself, will go to see the cause of the disturbance.

Upon this image of the queen moving majestically, if with mixed feelings, into the dark hallway, Dumas interrupts the narrative. Stepping back in time and ahead in space, he relates to the reader what actually occurred when Maurevel arrived in Henri's apartments—the resistance offered by Henri's loyal manservant, Orthon, the violent battle with most of the assailants killed, the escape of De Mouy:

[He] . . . arrived at the gate, gave the password, and leaped through, shouting:

"Get up there! They're killing someone at the king's orders!"

And, taking advantage of the surprise produced by his words as well as the two pistol shots, he ran off, disappearing without a scratch, into the rue du Coq.

It was precisely at this moment that Catherine had stopped her captain of the guards by saying, "Stay here. I shall see myself what is going on down there."

With this transition, the reader is again back in the chapter's central narration and sees through Catherine's eyes what she discovers, step by step, as she enters the now silent rooms; as she finds and questions Maurevel, whose larynx has been pierced so that he can utter no word; as she learns—or guesses—what has happened and tries to understand how her scheme has failed. Slowly she returns to her room, sure only that the hand of God or of fate is protecting Henri.

"What was the matter, Madame?" asked all those present except Madame de Sauve, who was too frightened to frame a question.

"Nothing," answered Catherine: "Just noise, that's all."

"Oh!" Madame de Sauve cried out suddenly, pointing to where Catherine had walked. "Your majesty says that nothing is wrong, and yet each of her steps leaves a stain on the carpet."

Thus holding the main action in suspense while he narrates what has happened offstage and letting his reader know what his characters can only surmise, Dumas maintains tension to the end and preserves the dramatic unity of the episode.

The conflicts and situations introduced in the first dozen chapters establish the framework of plot for the rest of the novel. All important characters, similarly, are introduced early. Dumas develops his characters in typical fashion, through action and dialogue rather than through analysis, but he often succeeds in conveying a greater depth and complexity than his detractors are willing to admit. Charles IX, for example, emerges as a surprisingly complicated individual: cruel yet capable of tenderness, weak yet capable of strength; sometimes transparent, sometimes enigmatic. Though less fully drawn, his brother François, duc d'Alençon, also appears in some depth. Dumas's depiction of François's jealousy and ambition, his intimations of the unhealthy side of the prince's nature and relationship to his sister are telling here and lay an effective groundwork for the villainous role he will play in the two succeeding novels.

Marguerite de Valois and Henri de Navarre, the heroic figures among the nobles, are not idealized as they might readily be, but they possess a great deal of charm and easily hold the sympathy of the reader. Though both are presented as ambitious and wily, they never appear really disloyal to the king and both project a sense of

genuine integrity. There is an interesting suggestion of real mutual
affection and desire for trust between Henri and Charles, who find
themselves so often forced because of conflicting interests not to
trust each other. Especially when completed by the portrait of the
same man twelve years later (in *Les Quarante-Cinq*), Henri stands
as one of Dumas's real successes at historical characterization. His
Marguerite is no less alive and vivid, though the woman recorded
by history is less fully reproduced by Dumas than is her husband.
On the other hand, Dumas most persuasively suggests that there
was perhaps more to Marguerite than history has been willing to
concede.

Alone of the major historical personages in the novel, Catherine
de Médicis seems unrelievedly flat and melodramatic, yet even she
is appropriately drawn for the role Dumas allots her. Hers is a
marvellously menacing presence in and behind the events of the
story. If her scenes with René, her perfumer, seem excessively
contrived to us today, there is still more than a little historical truth
in their evocations of superstition and black magic.

The two most engaging characters in the book, La Mole and
Coconnas, are also historical, but they are much more completely
Dumas's own creation. Adequately individualized by the simplest of
means—beginning with the characteristics conventionally ascribed
to their native provinces—they share their creator's verve, humor,
and vigor. While some of their love scenes with Marguerite and
Mme de Nevers verge on the ludicrous for modern readers, the
bond of friendship that develops between them in the course of
events stays utterly convincing. These two young men are the kind
of character Dumas seems most to admire and most successfully to
portray—young, passionate, energetic, and loyal—and their shared
conquest of love and glory is the situation he seems most happily to
depict. Their touching and tragic end, so unexpected and yet so
believable,[3] is perhaps the best demonstration of the skill with
which Dumas has built them.

In *La Reine Margot,* as in most of Dumas's novels, descriptive
passages rarely impede the flow of narrative or action. He sets
scenes and creates atmosphere with sureness and an impressive
economy of means. While he is likely to choose the obvious detail to
perform this task rather than the most subtle or distinctive one, his
choices are just and effective. Most often the description becomes
an integral part of the action itself. The account of the ceremonial

procession from the Louvre to view the decomposing bodies of Coligny and other massacred Huguenots, for instance, does advance the plot even though its principal function is unmistakably to evoke the way in which brilliance and picturesqueness coexisted with cruel grisliness and a strong taste for the macabre in the sixteenth century. Dumas's landscapes, like his city scenes, are almost never unpeopled unless the emptiness is significant, and an empty room or deserted street is almost always observed through the eyes of a character who comes upon it. Objects and places have no independent objective existence in Dumas such as they so often achieve in the great descriptions of Balzac, nor do they become personifications, almost living characters, as is the case with Hugo's Notre-Dame.

Humor seasons this work too. Inadvertent on a few occasions, most often it springs intentionally and naturally from character and situation, as much a function of Dumas's inborn exuberance as of his instinct for astutely deployed comic relief. There are a number of fully developed comic scenes in the novel, one of the most amusing of them found in Chapter XXXIII, where the king accidentally interrupts an intimate supper party in Marguerite's chambers. The stunned reactions of Gillonne, who admits the king, and of Marguerite and her guests—Mme de Nevers, La Mole, and Coconnas; the awkward flurry to conceal too late what cannot be concealed; the stumbling confusion after Coconnas upsets the table in order to extinguish the candles and mask the men's escape—all this is in the best tradition of farce.

For all its variety and complexity, however, *La Reine Margot* remains a clear and carefully constructed work. The many threads of plot alternate and mesh most satisfyingly, counterbalancing the choppy effect of many rapidly narrated events. The friendship of La Mole and Coconnas parallels their love affairs with Marguerite and the duchesse de Nevers and offers a contrast to the treachery and intrigue surrounding the activities of the king and his brother François. At the same time these sustained relationships supply a unifying force which pulls together the often separate concerns and actions of the characters. The sentimentality of the love scenes is set off against the black melodrama of Catherine's conniving and the violence of scenes of verbal or physical conflict. The counterplotting of Henri and Marguerite—joined by marriage, "political" alliance, and ambition; separated by love—builds suspense but seems somehow fresh and healthy in contrast to the villainy of their rivals and enemies. Battles, hunts, and scenes of pageantry in the court alternate strategically yet naturally with scenes on a smaller scale, whether of love or hate, friendship or intrigue.

The whole is symmetrically composed, framed by the cruel massacre scenes at the beginning and the still more cruel execution at the end with its brief but grim epilogue. The deaths at the end, however, in contrast to those at the beginning, have much more the quality of personal, intimate tragedy. The gradual shift of tone in the later episodes, the disappearance of humor and the sense of adventure, the emergence of deeper, quiet heroism all contribute to the effect of a steady progression within this balanced framework.

II   La Dame de Monsoreau

La Dame de Monsoreau is probably the most read of the novels in the Valois cycle. It is certainly the most ambitious. Yet despite its many strengths it fails in a number of respects.

It is ambitious, first, in scope. Dumas's triple intention is to present in depth a portrait of King Henri III against a detailed panorama of court and provincial life; to explore the intrigues and power struggles of the House of Lorraine; and to retell a well-known tale of love and betrayal—the same tale that he had used in *Henri III et sa cour*.

It is ambitious also in its form. Backgrounds are drawn more extensively than is often the case with Dumas. The actors are seen not only in the palace, the private mansions, and the streets of Paris, but against the forests and castles of Anjou and Touraine, and amid the pomp of royal pilgrimages to the convent of Sainte-Anne and the cathedral of Chartres. The number and variety of characters is correspondingly large, and two of Dumas's most memorable ones make their first appearance here: Chicot, Henri III's jester and confidant; and the Rabelaisian monk Gorenflot. The action ranges from spectacular balls to intimate love scenes, from conspiratorial gatherings in a convent to boisterous feasting at inns, from religious festivals to ambushes and duels.

In structure too *La Dame de Monsoreau* has a grander scheme than usual. Dumas seems to strive more consciously to utilize the technical resources at his disposal: symmetry and contrast; humor, exaggeration, and irony; multiple plot lines and more varied handling of time. Though the familiar basic situations and devices are not missing—the ravishing unknown beauty nursing the wounded hero back to health, the hero's loyal friend, the plots that misfire, the consistent villainy of the hero's arch rival—they are varied ingeniously and are interspersed with much that is fresh. Further, by sustaining single episodes over several chapters Dumas gives greater breadth and scale to the architecture of the novel, minimizing the impression of rush and an unbroken series of curtain lines. In sum, the book possesses great solidity as well as richness; to this degree Dumas has fulfilled his ambitions.

Yet some of the elements contributing to this richness and solidity are among the very factors preventing Dumas's complete success. One of the most evident weaknesses of the book is its length, which is excessive in terms of the ratio of size to substance. The title story, the unhappy love of Diane de Méridor and Bussy d'Amboise, is too simple and unproductive of real, integral complication to be stretched to the length that Dumas has stretched it. Furthermore, because it is fundamentally unrelated to the other major plot line—the activities of the Ligue and Chicot's efforts to help Henri III be the king he is supposed to be—the novel's unity suffers. Bussy's involvement in both spheres of action does not suffice to tie them together. His rivalry and duels with Henri III's *mignons*, for example, in no way bear on his relationship with Diane beyond the fact that he might be killed; and the duc d'Anjou's jealousy, which leads to his denunciation of Bussy, is of little consequence to the king.

Dumas's more extended descriptions and the largely digressive chapters that detail Henri III's character and behavior all interrupt the narrative more than they advance it and underscore the slightness of the plot material. Though there is no lack of surface interest in the characters and the historical color, only Henri and, to some extent, Chicot offer real depth of characterization in these sections. A final specific flaw, related to Dumas's attempt to vary his customary third person chronological narration, lies in the monologue of Diane de Méridor in which she recounts to Bussy the story of her life and misfortunes up to the night on which she, in effect, saved his life. Her narrative is weak because it is detailed to the point of tedium—a rarity in Dumas—and decidedly less than convincing. Not only does Dumas tax his reader's patience, he asks

him to accept as spontaneously told in conversation a tale that fills
four chapters, running to sixty closely printed pages. This is surely
one of Dumas's most clumsy expositions.

The central action of the novel is the love story of Bussy
d'Amboise, a young, handsome, and wealthy gentleman in the
service of the duc d'Anjou, and Diane de Méridor, the lovely but
unhappy wife of the strange comte Bryan de Monsoreau, newly
appointed *grand veneur du roi*. Abducted by the duc d'Anjou,
Diane had been rescued by the comte de Monsoreau; at her father's
insistence Diane agreed to accompany her rescuer to Paris and
marry him there. Then Diane meets Bussy and they fall in love; the
rest of the story is essentially their struggle to conceal this love from
Diane's husband and from the still-pursuing duc d'Anjou, ironically
the person to whom Bussy owes his loyalty. The duc d'Anjou's
discovery of their love leads to his betrayal of them and the final
tragedy.

Parallel to this plot runs the account of how several members of
the House of Lorraine—Henri, duc de Guise; his brother, the duc
de Mayenne; and their sister, Mme de Montpensier—attempt to
use the church, political intrigue, and military force to overthrow
Henri III. Their efforts, often helped by the monarch's weakness,
are ultimately foiled through the intelligence, bravery, and
foresightedness of the jester, Chicot.

The only real link between the two plots is the duc d'Anjou, who
extricates himself from a compromising involvement with the Ligue
by revealing to the comte de Monsoreau what he has discovered
about the count's rival for his wife's affections. The duke thus
becomes the dominant character in the novel as well as its villain.
He is also the only major figure from *La Reine Margot* to reappear in
La Dame de Monsoreau, if one excepts incidental glimpses of
Catherine de Médicis and Henri de Navarre. As presented here by
Dumas, François does not change or develop in any important way
from the duc d'Alençon portrayed in the earlier novel.
Sensuality, weakness, and selfishness remain his chief
characteristics; he differs only in attaining a far greater degree of
corruption and cruelty and in showing no redeeming qualities
whatsoever. In this last François resembles his mother in *La Reine
Margot*, even though as a whole his portrait seems less near to
caricature than did that of Catherine.

His brother, Henri III, is revealed as a much more complex

person. Dumas obviously revels in depicting his idiosyncrasies and
foibles of dress and grooming, his emotionality and childish fears,
yet he also conveys moments of insight, intelligence, and genuine
regal pride. Though Henri is shown without flattery Dumas does
not mock him either. Particularly because Chicot, for all his sarcasm
and irony, clearly loves and respects his king, the reader also tends
to see him through Chicot's eyes, with a degree of sympathetic
understanding to temper the full awareness of Henri's defects and
errors.

Chicot and Gorenflot, as we have already observed, are the most
striking characters introduced in this novel and they rank among
Dumas's great creations. Gorenflot, a monk of the order of Sainte
Geneviève, is the only important character who has no historical
counterpart; but, as little would have been known to Dumas about
the real Chicot, he also is, in effect, a fictional character beyond the
Gascon origins and the qualities of intelligence, wit, and courage
attributed to him by history as well as by the novelist. Together
Chicot and Gorenflot are responsible for much of the novel's humor,
the slyness and irony of Chicot making an entertaining contrast to
the broad comedy deriving from Gorenflot's stupidity and the
grotesque exaggerations of his gluttony and false piety. Occasionally
these exaggerations strain the reader's sense of the ridiculous, but
Chicot is unfailingly believable and the episodes in which he figures
are always alive and diverting.

Among the curious half-successes of this novel must be placed its
nominal hero and heroine, Bussy d'Amboise and Diane de Méridor.
It is hard to explain exactly why this should be so, especially in the
case of Bussy who seems in so many ways a perfect representative of
the Dumasian hero type. Handsome, intelligent, charming, and
brave, Bussy epitomizes the *jeune premier* of historical romance.
His sense of honor never tarnishes. He is capable of almost
superhuman feats of strength and valor. He is tender and faultlessly
devoted to his lady love. Yet for all this he remains remote—
admirable more than lovable. It has been suggested[4] that perhaps
Bussy strikes the reader this way because he already possesses the
qualities and has already achieved the reputation that Dumas's
greatest heroes are shown in the process of acquiring. This is
certainly one reason for the impression Bussy makes, but when he is
compared with the young heroes of *La Reine Margot* or with
d'Artagnan his lack of humor is also noted immediately. He is

beyond making blunders, and both he and Dumas consistently take him rather too seriously. Without being a stick-in-the-mud or a prig, Bussy seems as incapable of the lightheartedness of La Mole and Coconnas as he would be of errors and miscalculations like theirs.

Bussy also differs from Dumas's other heroes with respect to his friendships. Except for the few chapters early in the book where Bussy and Remy Le Haudouin cement their mutual affection and loyalty, and a few glimpses of the already established bond between Bussy and Saint-Luc, we do not have the character revelation and the evidences of personal warmth that accompany such accounts of developing *camaraderie* as we find in *La Reine Margot* and *Les Trois Mousquetaires*. However sincere the mutual esteem of Bussy and Remy, it remains a bond between social unequals; and we see for the most part results rather than causes of the friendship between Bussy and Saint-Luc.

Much the same may be said of Diane. She cannot be faulted as a Romantic heroine—and that is her greatest weakness as a character. She is unrelievedly beautiful, poised, noble, and long-suffering. She has none of the earthiness and wit of a Marguerite de Valois, nor does she share Marguerite's force and initiative. Throughout this novel she remains a passive figure; interestingly, she achieves more life in *Les Quarante-Cinq* where her role is smaller but more active. Together Diane and Bussy are reminiscent of Raoul de Bragelonne and Louise de La Vallière, though less in personality than in the way Dumas has presented them. It is he who assures us repeatedly of the virtues of these four characters—their beauty, sensitivity, and valor—rather than they who convince us of them dramatically.

III   Les Quarante-Cinq

The Forty-Five is one of Dumas's most absorbing and satisfying novels. It is a true sequel to *La Dame de Monsoreau* in that a majority of the principal characters first appeared in the earlier work and the story of Diane de Monsoreau and the duc d'Anjou works out to its conclusion only at the very end of this novel. This story is not its real focus, however. Here the center of attention and action is Henri III—his growing sense of his kingship, the efforts of his rivals and enemies to unseat him, and the efforts of the loyal Chicot and the variously motivated *mignons* and guardsmen to support him. Though plot lines often ramble and the action concentrates increasingly on the fate of the duc d'Anjou and Diane de Monsoreau

in the last section of the book, Henri III's position as the common
element in all the plots and subplots ultimately gives the work a
unity not achieved in *La Dame de Monsoreau.*

The action of *Les Quarante-Cinq* takes place between 26 October
1585 and 10 June 1586. The events to which Dumas assigns these
dates—the execution of Salcède and the death of the duc d'Anjou—
in actual fact occurred three and two years earlier respectively. His
reason for thus altering history was presumably to bring these
events into conjunction with the founding of "The Forty-Five"—
Henri III's personal guard—in 1585, though these changes are more
conspicuous than the converse would have been. His reasons for
making poison instead of tuberculosis the cause of the duc d'Anjou's
death are much more readily apparent. Yet in the end, as so often,
the liberties that Dumas takes with such recorded facts are much
less important than the success with which he has retained the flavor
of the period and events he recounts and the essence of the
historical personalities he depicts. The vignettes of the life of the
forty-five guardsmen in their quarters in the Louvre, for example,
are vivid and convincing, though many of the details must have
been invented. Moreover, the narrative is filled with intriguing
"historical probabilities" like the introduction of Jacques Clément,
the future assassin of Henri III, as a young monk in the Dominican
priory so prominent in the plotting of the Ligue.

The sharply individualized figures of Loignac, Ernauton de
Carmainges, and Sainte-Maline among the guardsmen add further
to the richness of texture of the novel, being at once colorful,
appealing, and historically appropriate. The two Joyeuse brothers
and d'Epernon—Henri III's other favorite—are characterized with
comparable art. Gorenflot reappears, more splendidly Rabelaisian
than ever. While the duc d'Anjou and the members of the Guise
family seem little developed from the preceding novel, they carry
out their function adequately and their relative flatness does not
diminish the general impression that in this novel Dumas has
achieved much more effective characterization of minor figures than
he did in *La Dame de Monsoreau.*

It is with the major characters, however, that Dumas reaches his
greatest heights. Henri III is even more forcefully depicted than he
was in *La Dame de Monsoreau* and this Henri de Navarre forms a
superb complement to the Henri of *La Reine Margot.* The qualities
of the man and king seen here enlarge, with both psychological and

historical consistency, the character presented in the earlier work. Bravado and shrewdness are transmuted into maturer courage and intelligence; conviction and intellectual bravery, rather than youthful vigor, triumph over the resistance of a body no longer wanting to go into battle. The picture of Henri de Navarre in this novel alone should give the lie to those who claim Dumas to be incapable of imparting true psychological depth and complexity to his characters; the case is even stronger when the two portraits of Henri are juxtaposed to reveal the evolution which Dumas has traced so well.

What is true of the character of Henri de Navarre is even more true of Chicot, who is the greatest and most memorable of the numerous great and memorable characters in this novel. Appearing first in disguise as Robert Briquet, *bourgeois de Paris*, he delights the reader continuously by his wit, perspicacity, and irony, his inventiveness and imagination, even as he dazzles by his physical strength and courage and endears himself by his integrity, loyalty, and humanity. The triumph of this novel, Chicot unquestionably belongs among the select group of Dumas characters headed by d'Artagnan who achieve a life and reality that go far beyond the facts of history or the limits of the novels in which we encounter them.

From the opening description of the throng at the Porte Saint-Antoine waiting to be admitted to the city, through the account of the public execution of Salcède, the splendid battle of Cahors led by Henri de Navarre, and the naval battle led by Admiral Joyeuse off Antwerp, *Les Quarante-Cinq* is filled with magnificent panoramas and scenes of mass action that surpass even the graphic and terrifying massacre of St. Bartholomew's Day in *La Reine Margot*. Yet perhaps the most striking passage in the entire book is that in which Dumas describes almost the exact opposite of such violent, heavily peopled battle scenes: the deserted plains of northern Belgium, traversed in eerie silence by three lone figures on horseback—Diane de Monsoreau, the faithful Remy, and young Henri de Joyeuse—who only gradually become aware of the menace behind the strange emptiness they encounter there. With masterly control Dumas evokes awe giving way to horror and terror as the muffled roar of approaching water grows louder and eventually sweeps everything before it in the full fury of the flood. It would be hard to imagine this episode narrated with more simple but appropriate means or with more telling effect.

The inequalities found in *Les Quarante-Cinq* do not lessen the power and worth of its finest pages, which stand among Dumas's best, or keep it from being the finest artistic achievement of the three novels in this series. As sequel to one novel and predecessor of another that was never written, *Les Quarante-Cinq* is less able than either *La Reine Margot* or *La Dame de Monsoreau* to be read independently. Yet because of its many links with the earlier books, the power of its characterizations, and its vision, it contributes most to the unity and the stature of the Valois cycle as a whole.

CHAPTER 7

The Marie-Antoinette Romances

THIRD in popularity among Dumas's cycles of historical novels, the series of romances covering the reign of Louis XVI and the French Revolution was also the last undertaken. It is the longest of the three and its publication spanned nearly ten years, the appearance of its final volumes in 1854–55 closing the great decade of historical novels that had begun with *Les Trois Mousquetaires.*

I *Substance*

Four novels relate the story of Marie-Antoinette from her arrival in France to marry the dauphin until the royal family's flight to Varennes in 1791: *Mémoires d'un Médecin: Joseph Balsamo (Joseph Balsamo* or *Memoirs of a Physician); Le Collier de la Reine (The Queen's Necklace); Ange Pitou (The Taking of the Bastille);* and *La Comtesse de Charny.* Commonly grouped under the general title *Mémoires d'un Médecin,* these books form a continuous work that traces major steps in the history of the years 1770–91.

Joseph Balsamo covers the period 1770–74—the closing years of the reign of Louis XV, whose death concludes the novel. Marie-Antoinette arrives from Austria to marry the dauphin and finds herself in a court seething with rivalries and intrigues. Mme Du Barry connives to win formal presentation at the court and, with the duc de Richelieu, schemes against the powerful duc de Choiseul. The mysterious Joseph Balsamo, later called the comte de Foenix, also becomes a party to the intrigues at Versailles. Simultaneously he is involved with the prorevolutionary activities of the Freemasons and is conducting experiments in alchemy and hypnotism. These experiments bear on his broader social and scientific aims but have serious immediate consequences for his wife Lorenza and Andrée de Taverney, both of whom he uses as mediums. At one point, having put Andrée in a trance, Balsamo is called away by an emergency and fails to release her. Young Gilbert finds Andrée in her unconscious state and rapes her. Subsequently he abducts the son she bears and leaves him in the care of Mme Pitou in the village of Haramont when he sets off for America.

Le Collier de la Reine takes place a decade later, in 1784–85. The action centers on the scandal of the diamond necklace engineered by the Countess Jeanne de la Motte-Valois—in which Balsamo is also involved, this time under his most famous pseudonym, Cagliostro—and Marie-Antoinette's love affair with the Swedish count Axel Fersen, here transformed into an imaginary French aristocrat, Olivier[1] de Charny. Dumas embroiders reality freely, but the central concerns remain historically valid. The affair of the necklace compromises the queen's reputation despite her innocence; her still platonic love for Charny does not go unobserved and gives rise to ugly rumors. In a desperate move to forestall further damage to Marie-Antoinette's honor, Charny and Andrée are married at the end of the novel.

The action of *Ange Pitou* occurs entirely within four months in 1789. It begins with a digression from the mainstream of events as new characters in Villers-Cotterêts and Haramont are introduced, then quickly progresses to the assault on the Bastille Among the prisoners released from the infamous prison is Gilbert—now Dr. Gilbert, the physician of the series title. Upon his return from America where he had been involved in the American Revolution, Gilbert had been imprisoned on the grounds of a *lettre de cachet;* it had been signed by the queen at the request of Andrée, who is still possessed of a bitter hatred of her betrayer. After his release Gilbert becomes one of the king's most trusted advisers. Marie-Antoinette, however, distrusts him and is, moreover, torn by jealousy as she observes Charny, five years after his marriage, now apparently finding Andrée's charms greater than hers. The novel ends abruptly with the royal family about to return under duress to Paris. The destinies of Andrée and Charny, Gilbert and his son Sébastien, Ange Pitou and his beloved Catherine Billot work themselves out in *La Comtesse de Charny* against a background of intensified social upheaval and violence, climaxing in the abortive flight to Varennes in 1791.

A fifth novel, *Le Chevalier de Maison-Rouge*, though not a part of the series[2], completes the story of Marie-Antoinette, treating her imprisonment and plots to save her from execution. While the portrait of Marie-Antoinette here does not significantly enrich that found in *Mémoires d'un Médecin*—it is quite conventionally idealized—the novel is one of Dumas's most gripping, and its splendid evocation of Paris under the Terror makes it a fitting and effective sequel to the cycle as well as absorbing reading in its own right.

II *Structure*

Despite the length of the series and the inevitable digressions as Dumas follows the many different groups of characters and works his way through the maze of subplots, the broad lines of structure remain clear and there are many indications that the four novels were conceived as a unit, unlike those making up the other two cycles. The fictional characters—Andrée de Taverney and her brother, Gilbert and his son—are rarely long absent from the reader's attention; should historical events form a neat conclusion at the end of one novel (e.g., *Joseph Balsamo*), the fate of these characters remains unresolved to open the way to the next. Among the historical personages, Marie-Antoinette and Louis XVI figure in all the novels and Joseph Balsamo in three of them, their lives running parallel or in contrast to those of the imaginary characters when not directly interwoven with them. References to events in other novels and anticipations of things yet to happen also reveal the planned unity of the series. Ange Pitou, for example, is introduced as a little child at the end of *Joseph Balsamo* when Gilbert places his son with the Pitou family before leaving for America. The entire *Collier de la Reine* and a lapse of fifteen years in the lives of these characters intervene before they reappear and Dumas exploits the situation he has set up, but the groundwork has been laid. Similarly, the parts played by Nicole Legay/d'Oliva and Beausire in *Le Collier de la Reine* are prepared by their appearance earlier in imaginary roles.

In scope and movement, too, the four novels emerge clearly as one. Though they may seem at first to digress or to serve merely as a foil for the pictures of court and city life, the country episodes in *Ange Pitou* and *La Comtesse de Charny* in fact do much more. They remind us that the peasants depicted here, however removed they may seem from the great issues of the day, were also a part of eighteenth century society and the movement that changed it. In contrast to Gilbert, Ange Pitou does not rise from his humble origins to become a wise counselor of kings and apostle of humane reason, but if his role is passive, his life and world are no less shaken and altered by the agony of the Old Régime. And finally, as the series progresses, the intervals of time between the novels become shorter and the action within them more concentrated, heightening the impression that the coming of the Revolution is a single, continuing movement that steadily gains momentum. There is an exceptional unity of vision, a perception of all the characters as direct participants in this approaching cataclysm, of all events and conflicts as steps toward it.

III   *Atmosphere and Tone*

The Marie-Antoinette romances contain no single character or group of characters as winning and memorable as d'Artagnan and his friends, or as Marguerite de Valois, Henri de Navarre, or Chicot. Where they fully equal the earlier cycles is in atmosphere, the re-creation of a period and its particular flavor. In the eighteenth century Dumas sees first the paradoxes and contrasts of an era at once enlightened and full of darkness, then the emergence of social forces and great principles that, with growing speed and violence, combine to rip the old society apart. Intrigues and corruption in every class, the frantic search for pleasure and personal gain, sensuality and vice on the one hand; on the other, preoccupation with great questions of philosophy and noble social aims, devotion to science (even pseudoscience), the ascendancy of reason over instinct—all these permeate the cycle.

The plotting of Mme Du Barry, her brother, and the duc de Richelieu, the licentiousness and deceitfulness of the blue-blooded Jeanne de la Motte, and the grasping ambition of the baron de Taverney find their lower-class counterparts in the dishonesty and coarseness of Andrée's maid Nicole, her lover Beausire, and the would-be thieves of the diamond necklace. The passion of all these characters for wealth, power, and status erases real distinctions of birth or class as they strive to manipulate persons and events for their own profit. The nobler motives of the Masonic brothers do not preclude their need also for secrecy and covert action, any more than the worthy ends of the peasants and bourgeois in revolt fore-stall their use of violent means to achieve them. The superficial brilliance, the elaborate etiquette of court life under both Louis XV and Louis XVI barely mask the undercurrents of hostility and self-seeking, of envy, speculation, and malice that are never far from the surface at balls and presentations, at a sleigh-ride on the frozen *pièce d'eau des Suisses* at Versailles, or in the simplest movement or gesture observed unawares. The obsession with pleasure that creates the visual delights of Versailles and Du Barry's castle at Luciennes (Louveciennes) extends itself to other sensations as well: Dumas endlessly notes extravagant dress and coiffures, perfumes, exotic diversions and rare, delicate foods, and the caressing or lascivious glances that linger on lovely bodies half-revealed in discreet *déshabillé*.

The devices by which Dumas creates the mysterious, conspiratorial atmosphere of the Masonic scenes in *Joseph Balsamo* are familiar ones, as are the techniques he employs to build dramatic tension in chases and confrontations or to accumulate suspense as a climax approaches. A different facet of his evocative power is revealed in an aspect of *Mémoires d'un Médecin* which has no real parallel in either the sixteenth or seventeenth century cycles and which, for that reason alone, obviously constitutes an important element of his view of the eighteenth century: its pervasive sensuousness and sophisticated eroticism. Sophistication, like subtlety, is not a quality ordinarily ascribed to Dumas, yet in these novels he does achieve and convey at will the air of conscious *polissonnerie* and sensuality, as well as the careful avoidance of excess, found in the paintings of Boucher and the sculptures of Bouchardon with which he decorates more than one scene. Among many possible illustrations of this point, none perhaps is better than Chapter 25 of *Le Collier de la Reine*. Entitled "Sapho," it is a short chapter containing almost no action, but it is so well placed and effective in its development of character and atmosphere that it gives no sense of digression or slowness.

In this chapter, returning from a masked ball at the Opéra, Mme de la Motte artfully rebuffs the frank advances of the cardinal de Rohan with promises of future nights and future pleasures they will share. She then dismisses all her servants, locks the doors, and slowly inspects every room, every object in her newly acquired residence with voluptuous delight:

Accustomed to solitude, sure of no longer being glimpsed even by a footman, she hastened from room to room, letting her light batiste *peignoir* float free in the drafts from under the doors that ten times in ten minutes exposed her charming knees.

And when she lifted her arms to open a cupboard, when her robe, slipping open, revealed the white roundness of a shoulder down to the point where the arm began, glowing with a rosy tint . . . then the invisible spirits, hidden beneath the hangings, sheltered behind the painted panels, must have rejoiced to have in their possession this charming mistress who believed that she possessed them. . . .

Jeanne felt her feet sink softly in the deep, thick wool of the carpet; her legs gave way and bent under her, a languor that was neither fatigue nor drowsiness pressed on her bosom and her eyelids with the delicacy of a lover's touch.

Dumas evokes other aspects of the times and the society in other ways. The seriousness with which he views Balsamo's quest for scientific truth lends credibility even to the charlatan's most fanciful achievements in the novel. Marie-Antoinette's visit to Mesmer's laboratory in the Place Vendôme introduces authentic historical detail through vivid description and drama. A leisurely pace and reflective tone color many of the long episodes in which Rousseau on his nature walks meditates to himself or aloud to a companion. The slightly tongue-in-cheek presentation of young Gilbert's philosophic pretensions becomes less marked as he matures under the guidance of the *promeneur solitaire*, and Gilbert's transformation and solid wisdom are accepted with complete seriousness in the last two novels. The overt struggles of the lower classes to obtain their human and civil rights—such events as the storming of the Bastille or the women's march on Versailles—are related with vigor and dramatic impact. But on the whole the characters in these books engage in far more debate, far more discussion of principles, than is ever the case in the action-filled earlier cycles. This difference too seems an expression of Dumas's idea of the age of enlightenment.

IV *Characters*

Whether intended as another reflection of Dumas's view of the period or simply an incidental result of the chosen plot, one other characteristic of the Marie-Antoinette cycle sets it apart from its two predecessors: the importance given in these novels to women. While there are of course prominent roles for men in this cycle, just as there were for women in the sixteenth and seventeenth century romances, it is clearly the women who dominate here, and neither of the earlier series offers such an imposing or varied female cast.

Marie-Antoinette and Mme Du Barry; the "austere and sinister"
Madame Louise de France—daughter of Louis XV—and Lorenza
Feliciani, the beautiful and tormented wife of Joseph Balsamo;
Andrée de Taverney and Nicole Legay move through the pages of
Joseph Balsamo. To this gallery *Le Collier de la Reine* adds Jeanne
de la Motte and *Ange Pitou* introduces the rosy-cheeked peasant girl
Catherine Billot, along with the minor but memorable *tante*
Angélique and Mme Billot, Catherine's mother. *La Comtesse de
Charny* introduces no new female characters but brings the long
story of Andrée de Taverney to its happy conclusion.

Marie-Antoinette is unquestionably the pivotal historical
character in this series of novels, however episodic her role may
sometimes seem. Her arrival in France is the first specifically
historical event in *Joseph Balsamo;* in its closing pages she is
proclaimed queen. Both historical and fictional actions center on her
in the next novel, and in *Ange Pitou* and *La Comtesse de Charny*,
though less constantly on the scene, she is still a strongly drawn,
impressive figure. Her evolution is traceable throughout the cycle.
Charming, naïve, frivolous as dauphine, as queen she remains
capable of tactlessness and foolishness as well as of anger and
jealousy; but deeper capacities for love, for courage, and for honest
self-assessment emerge gradually too. The queen often finds herself
at war with the woman as obligations conflict with desires, but
Dumas would have us believe that the inborn nobility of the queen
triumphs most often. Despite his obvious sympathy for Marie-
Antoinette and all the fictional elements he has had to introduce into
her role, Dumas's portrait of her remains true as well as generous.
His own evaluation of this portrait in the preface to *Le Collier de la
Reine* is accurate: he has avoided both the overidealization of her
admirers and the horrifying slanders of her enemies, with human
and convincing results.

Dumas's Mme Du Barry is likewise a balanced, essentially
accurate depiction that conveys her positive qualities as well as her
flaws with a justice and a justness not always achieved by others. His
Jeanne de la Motte is perhaps further from reality than either
Marie-Antoinette or Mme Du Barry, yet this too is a vivid, complex
portrait, tellingly drawn—and no more extraordinary than that
amazing woman herself.

Andrée de Taverney, like Marie-Antoinette, appears in all four novels; unlike the queen, though she ages she evolves scarcely at all as a character. A foil for the queen, Andrée is unwavering where Marie-Antoinette is vacillating, hypersensitive to the thoughts and opinions of others where the queen is indifferent or unobserving, obsessed with concealing her secret and preserving her honor at whatever cost. With her brother Philippe, Andrée is clearly intended to stand as a compendium of all the virtues that Dumas, for all his protestations of republicanism, always held to be inherently aristocratic.

The most important of the history-based male characters are Joseph Balsamo/Cagliostro and Jean-Jacques Rousseau. Balsamo's role in events is magnified and dramatized as is his personality; Rousseau is presented on a much more human scale in a realistic and convincing portrait. But the intrinsic interest of both these figures is complemented by a representative function. Balsamo stands for the brotherhood of Freemasons and for their role in the destruction of the notion of absolute monarchy, as Rousseau stands for a body of ideas. That Dumas has perceived these men in this way is more important to the novel than his taking at face value the image that the charlatan Cagliostro wished to project, than his exaggeration of the importance of the Masonic lodges in preparing the Revolution, or than his characteristic simplification and dramatization of philosophy.

Gilbert is the central nonhistorical male figure; his role too is both dramatic and representative. As Sigaux has pointed out,[3] Gilbert sets in motion the forces that determine the lives of the Taverney family and, through them, the Charny brothers and Ange Pitou. But he also synthesizes in himself what he observes at the court of Louis XV and what he learns at the feet of Rousseau, as well as the experiences—unspecified but obviously illuminating—of his years in America and his contact with the American Revolution. To borrow the words of Sigaux:

. . . when he becomes . . . the adviser of Louis XVI, he is not a puppet in the hands of the novelist but the symbol, or the voice, of a reason that spoke, actually, through other tongues. Gilbert did not exist: there were twenty Gilberts . . . they did not address to the king and queen the words that Dumas lends to Gilbert, but they were in the Estates General, in the philosophical societies and in the Masonic lodges; from there they spoke to the king and to the nation.[4]

Three other male characters merit special notice also—Olivier de
Charny, Ange Pitou, and Sébastien Gilbert. As we have remarked,
Charny is based upon the historical Count Fersen, lover of Marie-
Antoinette. Perhaps it would be more accurate to say that Dumas
assigns to an imaginary character some elements of the real Fersen's
role, notably the love affair and his part in the flight to Varennes.
Ange Pitou is historical in name only. Dumas rejected the real
Pitou, a royalist balladeer and pamphleteer, in favor of an honest
young peasant swept up in the turmoil of 1789. Dumas's Pitou is
drawn entirely from recollections of his own youth in Villers-
Cotterêts, as parallel details—and even whole passages—in *Mes
Mémoires* testify. But these characters too perform a double
function. Charny acts out his half-real, half-imagined role and aligns
himself with the Taverney brother and sister among those admirable
aristocrats for whom honor and personal loyalty mean more than
gain. Ange Pitou lives out his own life in the forests of Picardy and
the streets of Paris, but he is also every sincere and naïve convert to
the struggle for the rights of man who gets carried along by violent
events inconsistent with their alleged aims.

Apropos of Sébastien, Dumas writes in his preface to *La Comtesse
de Charny:* "There is young Gilbert, a composite of two natures that
were struggling at that time, that had been fusing for ten years, the
democratic element in which he takes after his father, the
aristocratic element he receives from his mother." The idea of the
fusion of these two elements is as central to this cycle as the
depiction of the events constituting the prelude to the Revolution
and its opening guns. It is Dumas's concept of the meaning and goal
of those events. It shapes the work as a whole and explains the
structure that we have seen him impose on his cast of characters.
They are not only individuals; they also systematically represent
various social groups and intellectual positions.

This much said, we must again remind ourselves that Dumas
remains a novelist after all. A comprehensive view of the Revolution
and a concern for symbolic or representative functions of characters
do not make him into either a historian or a philosopher. If such
fundamental differences as these in concept and structure, in tone
and characterization, separate the *Mémoires d'un Médecin* from the
d'Artagnan trilogy and the Valois cycle, the familiar qualities—and
faults—are still there, giving these romances the unmistakable
cachet of their author. The admirer of Dumas can approach this

cycle too expecting to find a full share of his most characteristic delights and equally characteristic surprises; he will not be disappointed.

CHAPTER 8

Fiction, Fact, and Collaboration

I *The History of France according to Dumas*

THE three cycles of romances we have just analyzed are justifiably the most popular and still most read of Dumas's historical novels; the judgment of his contemporaries and of posterity has been sound. This is not to suggest, however, either that alone they adequately represent what Dumas did with the materials of French history or that his other historical fiction is without merit. Some twenty to twenty-four additional novels fill in gaps between the periods covered in the cycles and extend their outer limits, back to the fourteenth century and ahead to the time in which Dumas was writing.

Only one novel by Dumas—*Le Bâtard de Mauléon*—treats the Middle Ages (1361–69). Five cover the sixteenth century from its beginning to the era of the religious wars: *Le Saltéador*, *Les Deux Diane*, *Ascanio*, *Le Page du Duc de Savoie*, and *L'Horoscope*. The most interesting of these are *Les Deux Diane* and *Ascanio*, both of which depict the reign of François Ier, though the action of the former (1521–74) extends through the reign of Henri II as well and overlaps, at the end, the period of *La Reine Margot*.

After the Valois cycle there is a gap of forty years left unexplored until *Les Trois Mousquetaires* (1625–28) opens the series of seventeenth century novels. The twenty years that Dumas skips between the first and second works in his Musketeer trilogy are partially filled by an unfinished novel, *Le Comte de Moret*. Published serially toward the end of Dumas's life, it did not appear in book form until after World War II. It is generally known today by the title *Le Sphinx rouge (The Red Sphinx)*, the reference being, of course, to Richelieu. The count of the original title is Antoine de Bourbon, a son of Henri IV who was killed at the age of twenty-five in the battle of Castelnaudary (1632). Because it was written too hastily it is an uneven book as well as an unfinished one, but it contains enough genuine interest and good writing to deserve to be better known. The same cannot be said of *La Guerre des Femmes (The Women's War)* which follows *Vingt Ans après* chronologically and, like it, deals with the Fronde; this is tedious and uninspired hack work. *La Tulipe noire (The Black Tulip)* can be loosely attached to Dumas's "history" of seventeenth century France though, as its title implies, the action takes place in Holland (1672–75). It is a pleasantly diverting tale known to many generations of first-year French students but of no great significance in Dumas's work.

The last years of the reign of Louis XIV, the Regency, and the beginning of the personal reign of Louis XV form the background of four novels: *Sylvandire, Le Chevalier d'Harmental, Une Fille du Régent (The Regent's Daughter)*, and *Olympe de Clèves*. All of these novels offer enjoyable reading, especially the best of them—*Le Chevalier d'Harmental*—which we have already noted as the first of the Dumas-Maquet collaborations. Another forty-year break occurs between the end of *Olympe de Clèves* (1729) and *Joseph Balsamo*. The series of Marie-Antoinette romances is partially overlapped by a pair of posthumously published novels of limited value and interest, *Le Docteur Mystérieux (The Mysterious Doctor)* and *La Fille du Marquis (The Marquis's Daughter)*, whose action falls between 1789 and 1795. The series is completed, after *Le Chevalier de Maison-Rouge*, by two important and absorbing novels: *Les Blancs et les Bleus (The Whites and the Blues)* and *Les Compagnons de Jéhu (The Company of Jehu)*. Both inspired by Charles Nodier's *Souvenirs et Portraits de la Révolution*, the former covers the period 1793–99 while the latter treats insurrections in southeastern France in 1799–1800 and the execution of four young members of the "Company of Jehu" at Bourg-en-Bresse. *Les Blancs et les Bleus* was the last historical novel published by Dumas during his lifetime; it stands as an impressive tribute to Nodier, whose friendship had lasted two decades (until his death in 1844) and whose influence on Dumas was lifelong.

Two other novels, *La San-Felice* and *Emma Lyonna*, relatively unknown but much admired by those who have read them, also depict the years 1798–1800. Like *La Tulipe noire* they are only indirectly related to the history of France: they evoke the period of French occupation and revolutionary struggles in Naples. The marchesa Luisa di San Felice was a Neapolitan aristocrat executed for conspiracy during those tumultuous days; Lord Nelson and Lady Hamilton (*née* Emma Lyon) are the other principal characters. Sometimes printed as one novel in two parts, this rich and colorful work was written by Dumas without collaborators.

The four "historical" novels that Dumas has devoted to nineteenth century subjects are among his less successful works, though *Les Mohicans de Paris* enjoyed a spurt of popularity when it inspired a French television series and was reissued in the *Livre de Poche* edition. It takes place in the 1820's; the bizarre title refers to a group of revolutionary conspirators under the Restoration. *La Terreur prussienne,* written and set in 1866, is less a novel of contemporary history than a remarkable foreshadowing of the future, as events four years later were to demonstrate. The other nineteenth century titles are *Salvator* (sequel to *Les Mohicans de Paris*), and *Les Louves de Machecoul (The She-Wolves of Machecoul)*.

It is less surprising to find unevenness and a few failures in this vast undertaking than it is astonishing to note the general level of achievement and the number of successes. As we have seen repeatedly, one does not—one should not—come to this *oeuvre* for factual, systematic historical information, but it remains a work of history as well as of fiction. On the whole Dumas simplifies but does not falsify the portraits he draws of great historical personalities. Similarly his liberties with chronology do not seriously distort the depiction of great events or lessen the fundamental accuracy of his evocations of period atmosphere. When reading Dumas one knows what it felt like to live through the St. Bartholomew's Day massacre, to be involved in the Fronde, or to live in the fishbowl of Louis XVI's Versailles. Because at his best he so thoroughly engages our interest and concern, Dumas succeeds in making us—again the phrase is Sigaux's—"contemporaries of his characters."[1] Their world becomes our world.

But most importantly, Dumas succeeds in his goal of making history popular in every sense of the word.[2] Rare indeed, we suspect, is the reader who lays down a Dumas novel without at least the impulse to learn more about its characters and period. Checking Dumas against "real history" becomes an extension of our pleasure in reading him that in no way detracts from it. Quite the contrary, such corrections of vision enrich the reality of both worlds—and demonstrate as well that each one needs the other.

II   *The Dumas Whodunit*

It is impossible to survey the mass of Dumas's historical fiction as we have done without facing a question that we have deliberately avoided up to this point, that of Dumas's collaborators. The matter is a complex one in which there can be no clear and definitive answers. Among the many scholars and critics who have come to grips with the problem, Henri Clouard and Gilbert Sigaux stand out for the judiciousness of their analyses and conclusions; it is to them first that we would refer the reader who wishes to pursue the question in depth.[3]

With respect to Dumas's plays, collaboration had never been an issue except in the prolonged fight between Dumas and Gaillardet over *La Tour de Nesle.* Joint effort was the order of the day in writing for the popular theater in the nineteenth century, and Dumas was no different in this from any of a dozen other successful playwrights. Moreover, the collaborators' names normally appeared beside his on the playbills—though not all of them found their way into Dumas's published *Théâtre complet*—and they all received their fair share of royalties. The nature and extent of the collaborations varied greatly, of course, but in evaluating the force and originality of Dumas's part it is only fair to bear in mind that his two most important and influential plays—*Henri III et sa cour* and *Antony*—are his own creations from initial idea to final line of text.

Dumas had never tried to make a secret of his use of collaborators in writing the novels any more than he had for his plays. When one looks at the list of publications that appeared over his name in 1844–45 alone, however, it is easy to understand that such output could cause disbelief among his contemporaries and give rise to rumors of ghost writers. The rumors took tangible and scurrilous form in 1845 with the publication of a pamphlet entitled *Fabrique de Romans, Maison Alexandre Dumas et Cie (Novel Factory: Alexander Dumas & Co.).* Its author Eugène de Mirecourt (the pen name of J.–B. Jacquot) in the most insulting way attacked Dumas personally and professionally, accusing him of taking advantage of collaborators who actually wrote his books for him and of buying manuscripts to which he then merely signed his name.[4]

Several of the collaborators—including Auguste Maquet—who were presented as Dumas's victims publicly disavowed Mirecourt's claims. The attack was censured by the Société des Gens de Lettres and Mirecourt was condemned by the courts to a fine and a prison

term. But the damage had been done. To this day Dumas's
reputation has suffered, at least indirectly, from Mirecourt. Though
the attack was discredited the fact of collaboration remained and,
with it, the uncertainty about what share of Dumas's works can fairly
be attributed to him and what must be credited to others.

The answer to that question, insofar as one can be said to exist,
must be sought in study of the limited documents that remain. The
first systematic attempt to do so was the work of Gustave Simon,
Histoire d'une collaboration: Alexandre Dumas et Auguste Maquet
(1919). Simon's questionable use of documentation and his strong
pro-Maquet bias produced conclusions that have been substantially
revised by later scholars. Without going into the details of their
research we may summarize as follows the views generally held
today with respect to Dumas and his collaborators on the novels.

Of the several that Dumas acknowledged—principally Maquet,
Paul Meurice, Paul Bocage, Paul Lacroix (the "Bibliophile Jacob"),
Cherville, and Dauzats—by far the most important one was
Maquet, who worked with Dumas on at least ten or twelve of the
most famous novels, including the three major historical cycles and
Le Comte de Monte-Cristo. Theirs was a genuine collaboration in
which ideas were discussed and developed together, not just one in
which Maquet gathered background material, worked out plot
structure, or prepared sections in draft form as Dumas requested
them, though he did some of all these things. Those of Maquet's
outlines and drafts that remain leave little doubt as to what Dumas
brought to the books in the actual writing—or that he in fact wrote
them. If the bones of plot and character are there in Maquet's
sketches, it is Dumas beyond question who provides the flesh and
blood—and the breath of life. He revises, expands, deletes, or
elaborates always with his infallible sense of pace and dramatic
effect, with the verve, humor, and excitement that are his alone. If
further evidence of the importance of Dumas's contribution is
needed, Clouard points out[5] that these same qualities abound in
Dumas's *Mémoires* and *Impressions de voyage,* works whose
authorship has never been disputed, while the novels published
independently by Dumas's collaborators "never rise above
mediocrity."

For a long time even those willing to concede this much to Dumas
maintained that in their collaborations Dumas was the writer and
Maquet the historian. This view too has been qualified by Sigaux,[6]

who points out that though Maquet (or others) may well have done some research for him, Dumas's own knowledge of history cannot be discounted. His historical compilations stand as concrete evidence that he knew his sources at first hand, and that the apt detail of historical color, the amusing touch, or dramatic anecdote more often than not was his discovery.

No single facet of the work, then, can be attributed exclusively to either Dumas or his collaborators, but the bulk of the evidence supports the belief that in most of the important ways and in all the essential ones Dumas is indeed Dumas. We can only conclude with Sigaux[7] that while Dumas might not have been able to write certain of his novels without his collaborators, without him none of the best ones could have been written at all. With that in mind, while giving due recognition to the part played by the collaborators in the creation of this great body of writings, it does not seem unjust to do as we have done and refer to the single or collective author as Dumas alone.

CHAPTER 9

The Chronicler of Romance:
Le Comte de Monte-Cristo

DURING a visit to Marseille in 1841[1] Dumas borrowed from the city library a copy—never returned—of Courtilz de Sandras' *Mémoires de Monsieur d'Artagnan*. In all probability this fortuitous happening planted the seed that ultimately produced *Les Trois Mousquetaires*. Another such casual, unplanned occurrence lies at the beginning of *Le Comte de Monte-Cristo*, the only book of Dumas's to challenge, if not to surpass, that novel in popularity. Dumas tells the story in one of his *causeries* written many years later, "*État civil du* Comte de Monte-Cristo" ("Vital Statistics on *The Count of Monte-Cristo*").[2]

Early in 1842 Dumas, who was then living in Florence, took the young Prince Napoleon to visit the island of Elba at the request of the prince's father, Jerome Bonaparte. After touring Elba they decided to go hunting on the nearby island of Pianosa. The peasant who carried their game bag assured them that the hunting would be better on yet another island, just visible on the horizon—the island of Monte-Cristo. Off they sailed the next morning to Monte-Cristo, but neither to land nor to hunt. Their rowers informed them as they were about to jump ashore that, the island being deserted, boats could not stop there without all who landed subsequently being quarantined for five or six days. The prince and Dumas debated the risks, then Dumas suggested:

. . . if Monseigneur is willing. . . . —What?—We will simply go around the island. —What for? —To fix its geographical position. After that we will go back to Pianosa. —It will be fine to pinpoint the location of the island of Monte-Cristo, but what good will that do? —It will enable me, in memory of this trip I have the honor of making with you, to give the name of the island of Monte-Cristo to a novel I shall write someday. —Then let's go around the island of Monte-Cristo, said the Prince, and send me the first copy of your book.

The novel remained no more than a name in the back of Dumas's mind for a year at least. In 1843 he contracted to write eight volumes of *Impressions de voyage dans Paris* for the publishers Béthune and Plon, but before he began writing M. Béthune came to inform him that they did not want a "historical and archaeological stroll through Caesar's *Lutèce* and Philippe Auguste's Paris." What the publishers now envisioned was a novel to compete with Eugène Sue's overwhelmingly successful serial *Les Mystères de Paris*, in which the Parisian "travel impressions" would be merely incidental.

The change was an easy one for Dumas to make. Searching for a plot, he recalled an anecdote from the police files that had intrigued him for several years and decided to use it as a starting point. Called *The Diamond and the Vengeance*,[3] it told the story of a low trick—a false denunciation—played on a poor shoemaker, François Picaud, as a consequence of which he was imprisoned for seven years. During his imprisonment Picaud served an Italian ecclesiastic who was also a political prisoner, then fell heir to an enormous fortune upon the Italian's death. The second part of the story recounts Picaud's systematic search, after his release from prison, for vengeance on those who had wronged him.

Dumas began his story in Rome, where a rich nobleman named the Count of Monte-Cristo did a great favor for a young French traveller. His recompense was to have the Frenchman serve as his guide when he in turn visited Paris. The trip to Paris, ostensibly to see the city (and to provide Dumas with the pretext for his *impressions*) was in reality to track down and punish enemies who had had the count imprisoned for ten years. When Dumas had written what now constitutes, with some alterations, Chapters 31–40—the Italian portion of the novel—he spoke of his work to Maquet. Maquet suggested that Dumas was skipping over the most interesting part of his hero's life by starting where he did and he pointed out the awkwardness of trying to fill in that much background material by flashbacks and narration. Dumas continues:

"You may be right," I said. "Come back for dinner tomorrow and we'll talk it over."

That evening, night, and next morning I had thought over his observation and it had seemed so right to me that it prevailed over my original idea. So when Maquet arrived the next day he found the work divided into three distinct parts: Marseille, Rome, Paris. That very evening we worked out together the outline for the first five volumes. . . .

The rest, without being completely finished, was almost all roughed out. Maquet thought he had just done me the favor a friend would do. I insisted that he had done a collaborator's job.

That is how *The Count of Monte-Cristo*, begun by me as travel impressions, turned gradually into a novel and ended up a collaboration between Maquet and me.

Fragments of the outline in Maquet's writing and letters exchanged between the two men illuminate their continuing active collaboration as they refined and elaborated characters, motivations, and details of action to produce the enormous structure of the completed novel. It was published serially over a year and a half, with several long interruptions for which Dumas invented impressive but vague excuses. In reality the delays were inevitable. During the entire time of composition and publication Dumas and Maquet were engaged in writing plays and other novels— sometimes three at once—together, while Dumas was writing and publishing still more alone, suing Eugène de Mirecourt, and planning his own Château de Monte-Cristo to be built at Port-Marly.

I   *Marseille, Rome, Paris*

The three sections into which Dumas divided his novel are unequal, but appropriately so. Part one, *Marseille*, contains thirty chapters; part two, *Italie*, which is really a bridge between the captivity and the vengeance, has nine noticeably longer chapters; the accomplishment of Monte-Cristo's vengeance in part three fills the remaining seventy-nine chapters (1040 pages in the Garnier edition).

Each of the three sections opens on a precise date—part one on February 24, 1815, as the three-master *Pharaon* sails into the port of Marseille under the command of Edmond Dantès, the nineteen-year-old first mate who had taken charge when the captain died at sea. Upon the orders of the dying captain Dantès had stopped at the island of Elba where he had delivered a letter to Murat, seen Napoleon, and been given a letter to deliver personally to the Bonapartist group in Paris. The owner of the ship, M. Morrel, welcomes Dantès warmly and promises that his captaincy will be made permanent before the ship sails again. By thus performing his duty and earning the respect of both shipmates and superiors Dantès sets up his happiness: he pays his elderly father's debts to a grasping neighbor, Caderousse, and plans an immediate wedding with his fiancée Mercédès. Unknowingly, by the same deeds he has prepared his downfall. His rival for Mercédès, Fernand, and the envious ship's accountant, Danglars, with the knowledge but not the active help of Caderousse, send a letter to the King's Prosecutor denouncing Dantès as a Bonapartist conspirator. Seized by the authorities in the midst of his prewedding party, Dantès is questioned by M. Noirtier de Villefort, the assistant prosecutor, who had been called away from his own engagement party to conduct the interrogation. At first sympathetic to Dantès, the ambitious and ultraroyalist Villefort is stunned to discover that the letter given Dantès to deliver in Paris is addressed to his own father—a *girondin* and Bonapartist whose political views Villefort finds intolerable. Fearful for his own position if word should leak out, Villefort reads and destroys the letter, swears Dantès to secrecy, then sends him off to solitary confinement in the Château d'If. There Dantès remains for fourteen years.

The rest of part one details Dantès' imprisonment, the tortures of his loneliness and ignorance of why he is there; his friendship with the abbé Faria[4] who not only tells him the secret of the treasure on the island of Monte-Cristo but gives him the incalculable wealth of learning; his near-miraculous escape, and his return to Marseille a transformed man. Now free and endowed with apparently inexhaustible riches and power, Dantès seeks to unravel the mysteries of his years of imprisonment. His father is dead; Mercédès has disappeared. In disguise he tracks down Caderousse and bribes him into revealing the story of the false denunciation, thus confirming his suspicions. In another disguise he intervenes to right the financial affairs of his former employer and friend Morrel, who had been driven near suicide by a series of disastrous reverses. At the end of part one a new *Pharaon* sails into the port—a duplicate to the last detail of the old vessel once captained by Dantès and recently reported down in a storm. His friends thus rewarded, Dantès is now ready to punish his enemies.

Part two takes place during the pre-Lenten carnival season in Italy in 1838. Before joining his friend Albert de Mortcerf in Rome for Mardi Gras, the young baron Franz d'Épinay decides to take a trip to Elba. From there he goes to Pianosa to hunt, but is disappointed and, like Dumas and Prince Napoleon, accepts his guide's suggestion to push on to the island of Monte-Cristo. They approach the island at night, see the campfires of presumed smugglers, but ascertain that they are friendly and—unlike Dumas and the prince—go ashore. Franz is invited to dine with the leader of the bandits and is escorted blindfolded into the sumptuously appointed caves of the Count of Monte-Cristo, who identifies himself as Sinbad the Sailor. (Franz in turn introduces himself as Aladdin.) Not only the names, but the entire episode seem drawn from the *Arabian Nights;* the description of the interior of the cave, the meal served by the mute slave Ali—everything is unreal, mysterious, and luxuriously exotic. After the meal Franz is given one of his host's hashish tablets and experiences a sort of opium dream, also described in vivid detail. When he awakes Franz is again on the shore and only "Sinbad's" boat on the horizon offers confirmation of the reality of what has happened.

In Rome, Franz and Albert become acquainted with the enigmatic Count of Monte-Cristo who occupies a suite in their hotel. Franz recognizes him as his host on the island but says nothing. The count shows the young men every kindness and it is to him that Franz turns for help when Albert is kidnapped by the notorious bandit Luigi Vampa. Instead of lending the ransom money that Franz asks for, Monte-Cristo goes with him to Vampa's hideout in the catacombs of San Sebastian and secures Albert's immediate release. Before leaving for Paris the next day Albert extracts a promise from the count that he will come to visit him at his home in Paris exactly three months hence, at 10:30 A.M. on May 21st.

Early in the third part it becomes apparent that not only are the sins of the fathers visited on their sons, but the sons are often the instruments of their fathers' punishment. Twenty-three years have elapsed since Dantès was sent off to prison and a new generation has matured, the lives of the young people entangled by threads from a past of which they are often unaware. Maximilien Morrel, son of Dantès' benefactor, is in love with Valentine, daughter of his enemy Villefort by his first marriage. Danglars has a daughter, and Albert de Mortcerf is the son of Mercédès and Fernand. The intricacy of the plot in this long section defies analysis, but a résumé would serve little purpose in any event. Suffice it to say that through all the web of often sordid relationships and family skeletons, Dantès relentlessly pursues his vengeance. Inexorably he prods fate, exposing past crimes or forcing their exposure, precipitating latent crises and catastrophes until again the innocent fall victim to the guilty and he wonders if he has gone too far. A final meeting with Mercédès ends in a final farewell. Dantès revisits the Château d'If. And at the novel's end Maximilien Morrel and Valentine de Villefort stand side by side on the island of Monte-Cristo, watching the count's ship as it disappears beyond the horizon.

II   *Art Imitates Life*

Le Comte de Monte-Cristo, we are frequently reminded, is not a historical novel but a *roman de moeurs*—a novel of manners. The story Dumas tells here was not remote from the first audience to which it was addressed; quite the contrary, the bulk of its action was placed squarely in contemporary times and in the city where most of its first readers lived. A fundamental concern, then, for Dumas and Maquet, was reconciling reality and fantasy so as to be convincing—and satisfying—on both levels. Let us look first at the realistic elements, those which justify calling this *Arabian Nights* adventure a novel of contemporary manners.

The most immediately obvious realism is in settings. From the opening scene on, especially in parts one and three, places are identified and identifiable. All the landmarks of the harbor at Marseille are named as the *Pharaon* approaches the port and passes them one by one, then streets and squares of the city as Dantès hastens first to see his father, then to the Catalan village to find Mercédès. The engagement dinner of Villefort and Mlle de Saint-Méran is located precisely "on the rue du Grand-Cours, opposite the fountain of the Méduses, in one of those aristocratic old houses built by Puget. . . . " As Dantès is escorted to prison, he recognizes with horror the Château d'If looming up from its rock in front of the boat. Descriptions are brief but, like references to places, concretely real. The same geographic precision, the same concreteness of detail and allusion characterize the description of Caderousse's Auberge du Pont du Gard (Chapter XXVI) and the *quartiers* and houses of Paris among which characters and action move in part three. Dumas rarely fails to specify not only the part of the city but street names and house numbers. Even the eerie, semihallucinatory episodes of the Italian section of the novel take place in manifestly real locations, be they the hotel of *maître* Pastrini on the Piazza di Spagna in Rome (both hotel and proprietor were personally known to Dumas), the carnival-filled streets, the moonlit Colosseum, or the island of Monte-Cristo itself.

Dumas's realism goes beyond geography, however; it extends to characters, events, and milieux as well. Other real persons besides *maître* Pastrini figure in the novel in imagined roles or by way of allusion: the imaginary Haydée, for example, is the daughter of the real Ali Pasha of Janina and is received in the Luxembourg palace by a real *Président de la Chambre des Pairs.* The text is filled with references to fashionable clubs and restaurants, to real newspapers, to artists and writers of the day, to operas and plays that were being performed. From all this, as from the parallel engagement parties on different levels of society, the balls and dinners of the rich, the financial struggles of the poor, the honest bourgeois life of the Morrels, the social-climbing of Villefort, the unsavory dealings of Caderousse and Cavalcanti, the politics and commerce, there emerges a rich and accurate picture of a society, a picture at once authentic and minutely familiar to the book's first public.

Maquet's notes reveal with what meticulous care the relationships and psychology of the characters were prepared so that this aspect of the book too would be convincing. Behavior is always believable without always being predictable. The avarice of Caderousse is established before he succumbs to the temptation of the false abbé Busoni's diamond. Fernand's role in the tragedy at Janina is consistent with the weakness of character he had demonstrated in 1815, just as the courage and force of character displayed by old Noirtier at the end are in keeping with all prior impressions of him. Danglars's cupidity motivates his participation in the plot against Dantès, dominates his family relationships, and produces both his financial success and his ultimate ruin. The shift of the opening action from 1807—the year of Picaud's imprisonment—to 1815 makes the denunciation of Dantès more immediately believable because it is political. Villefort's motivation is strengthened by the same change.

A final realistic element—though it may not at first seem to be one—is the plot, which is drawn, as we have seen, from a true story. Though Dumas has expanded the simple tale at every point, elaborated the characterizations and profoundly altered the outcome, the core of truth—as fantastic as any fiction—remains. We may suspect that it was to emphasize this aspect of the work that he had Peuchet's anecdote appended to his text in the second reprinting of 1846.

The realism of *Le Comte de Monte-Cristo,* far from making its fabulous elements seem less believable, makes them more so. They are firmly rooted in a reality so familiar as to be almost tangible. If the reader believes in this reality of setting and situations, if he finds the characters and motives human and credible, then he will be much more ready to accept the impossible as possible. At every point it is clear that Dumas is working from this assumption.

The fantastic is not only rooted in reality; it grows from it also. Dumas's procedure in adapting his source is quite consistently to magnify or exaggerate the ordinary in order to arrive at the extraordinary. The imprisonment of Picaud lasted seven years; Dantès is in the Château d'If for fourteen. The fortune to which Picaud fell heir—admittedly already more than ordinary—amounted to about eleven million francs in property, diamonds and cash, and was located in Milan; Dantès found at least ten times as much buried in the cave on the deserted island of Monte-Cristo. The rich Italian whom Picaud served in prison "less as a servant than as a son" became the abbé Faria, who not only possessed the secret of Monte-Cristo but was in every way an exceptional man, qualified to enrich Dantès intellectually and spiritually as well as materially. The disguises employed by Dantès are more numerous and varied than those used by Picaud in tracking down his enemies. Most striking of all, the humble shoemaker who devoted his life to avenging a wrong becomes a young man of promise transformed by his experience into a Promethean superman.

But the magnification occurs not only in such transformations; it is inherent in Dumas's manner of telling the story as well. One needs only to reread Chapter XXIV—in which Dantès finds the treasure—to see how a relatively simple narration, by its pacing and building up of detail, amplifies the action to a dimension consistent with the spectacular discovery at its end. Dantès himself cannot believe that he will find a treasure there, but step by step as the abbé Faria's words prove true, the reader—like Dantès—is forced to accept first the probability and then the reality.

Not all the fantasy in the novel, of course, thus grows from its factual source or from the realistic fictional context. The most conspicuously fabulous elements spring from Dumas's imagination and temperament. Dantès's remarkable escape from the Château d'If was Dumas's invention—at least it did not come from Peuchet—and it is worth noting that the part of the novel written by Dumas alone is the most heavily charged with romantic exoticism. In that section, starting from his personal experience—which he assigns to Franz d'Épinay—Dumas turns his imagination loose, revelling in the color of the Roman carnival, the mystery of moonlit ruins, the terror of bandits who strike by night. All this is, at bottom, quite conventional and in the vein of Hugo's *Orientales* and a whole body of literature of fifteen to twenty years before. But the barren rock of Monte-Cristo calls up more remote and personal memories, and he creates inside it a fabulous cavern from the *Arabian Nights* and a hero who, like the heroes of those tales, blends in his person power, wealth, and mystery.

In his introduction to the Garnier edition of the novel J.-H. Bornecque suggests that Dantès is a projection of Dumas's dreams, frustrations, and nature.[5] Relating him to the heroes of *Pauline* (1838) and *Georges* (1843), whom he finds to be less complete versions of the type fully embodied in Monte-Cristo, Bornecque argues that the personal qualities of Dumas that Monte-Cristo shares—for example, his love of the sea, his combination of humble origins and exceptional accomplishments—are only the starting point of the resemblance. Monte-Cristo realizes all his dreams, including the final affirmation of his rights and his superiority, in vengeance on his enemies and humiliation of his detractors; through Monte-Cristo, says Bornecque, Dumas vicariously shares this achievement. "Monte-Cristo, determined to conquer the impossible by force of will, is absolutely Alexandre Dumas as he sees himself or as he wishes himself to be."[6]

Bornecque's arguments are persuasive and his idea is both illuminating and suggestive. There are other comparisons to be made, however, which avoid the fascinating but tricky psychological identification of author and hero. Dantès may be examined in relation to others among Dumas's heroes such as Antony and Kean. Like them he is an *homme supérieur* who is a victim of society and the laws, prejudices, and hostility of lesser men than himself. Unlike Antony and Kean, Dantès is enabled to move above and beyond the limitations others would impose on him. Where both Antony and Kean ultimately have no choice but to yield to society as it exists, Edmond Dantès, Count of Monte-Cristo, successfully turns the forces of society to his own ends, against those individuals who have been its instruments in his life. For all the differences between them and between the authors, one can see a parallel as well between Monte-Cristo and Balzac's Vautrin, another superman. But where Vautrin's hostility, like Antony's, is directed against society as a whole, Monte-Cristo's is more specific. Where Vautrin does not hesitate at direct intervention to change the course of events (e.g., having Frédéric Taillefer killed in *Le Père Goriot*), Monte-Cristo operates more indirectly: his victims are made to become victims of themselves—of their own weaknesses of character; their own misdeeds. As Sigaux has pointed out in comparing Dantès and Picaud of *Le Diamant et la Vengeance*,[7] it is not insignificant that while Picaud—like Vautrin, we add—*takes* vengeance, Dantès *is avenged*. At the end justice is achieved and virtue is rewarded because good is ultimately stronger than evil, not merely because of Monte-Cristo's power. This optimistic conviction persists, overriding Monte-Cristo's doubts about his right to take unto himself the prerogatives of God and ringing forth in his final admonition to young Morrel and Valentine: "Wait and hope."

III   *Life Imitates Art*

Such a view of the world could only add to the appeal of a work already so attractive in its excitement, its surprises, and its value as sheer entertainment. If Monte-Cristo was a projection of Dumas's own dreams, he was surely even more the embodiment of the aspirations of a whole generation, just as the novel was an expression of the visible reality that generation knew. But the aspirations of that generation proved to be universal also. The success of *Le Comte de Monte-Cristo* was instantaneous, phenomenal, and enduring. Like *Les Trois Mousquetaires*, this novel has known no period of eclipse in popularity, still appearing in new editions with astonishing frequency and ageing scarcely at all. Its hold on the public imagination is as firm as ever and its hero has assumed a degree of reality for readers at least the equal of d'Artagnan's.

Indeed, if the historical d'Artagnan has become indissolubly merged with the fictional one, the fictional Monte-Cristo has become correspondingly "historical." Dumas transmuted something of the magical world of his novel into reality with his Château de Monte-Cristo at Port-Marly, though this dream was realized only briefly.[8] But almost as soon as the novel was published readers everywhere began seeking or inventing traces of the characters in the locales it described. Dumas wrote of this phenomenon in 1857, in the introduction to *Les Compagnons de Jéhu;* what he says there would be almost as true had he written it yesterday. Speaking of the importance he attaches to visiting the actual sites of events he writes about, he observes:

That gives such a quality of truth to what I write that the characters I plant sometimes grow where I have planted them, to the extent that some people end up believing they actually existed.

There are even people who claim to have known them.

So now I am going to tell you something in confidence, dear readers, but do not repeat it. I don't want to wrong the honest *pères de famille* who live by this little industry; but if you go to Marseille they will show you Morrel's house on the *Cours,* the home of Mercédès in the Catalan village, and the cells of Dantès and Faria in the Château d'If.

When I staged *Monte-Cristo* at the Théâtre-Historique I wrote to Marseille to have a drawing of the Château d'If made and sent to me. The drawing was intended for the stage designer.

The artist to whom I wrote sent the drawing I had requested, but he went further than I had dared to ask. Under the drawing he wrote: "View of the Château d'If showing the place from which Dantès was thrown." I have learned since that a good man attached to the staff of the Château d'If was selling fish-bone pens made by the abbé Faria himself.

The only problem is that Dantès and the abbé Faria never lived except in my imagination and that, consequently, Dantès could never have been thrown down from the Château d'If nor could the abbé Faria have made any pens.

But that is what comes of visiting localities.

CHAPTER 10

Other Fiction

THE first impression received from a survey of Dumas's other nonhistorical fiction is of its variety. The high-spirited *Le Capitaine Pamphile* (1839) combines pirates, Huron Indians, and exotic animals with happy results. A year before that book Dumas had published his first contemporary novel, *La Salle d'armes*— actually a pair of short novels of which the more memorable is the first, *Pauline.* A moving tale filled with Romantic antitheses, it is the story of a young woman in love with a man who turns out to be a thief and murderer. *Amaury* (1844) is another love story, while *L'Histoire d'un Casse-Noisette* (1845) is an adaptation from E. T. A. Hoffmann, the source of Tschaikowsky's ballet *The Nutcracker.* Hoffman is the hero of *La Femme au Collier de velours (The Woman with the Velvet Necklace),* perhaps Dumas's most successful venture into the literature of the occult. This is an eerie mingling of dream and reality, a story of Hoffmann's love for a dancer that is completely in the vein of such tales by the German master as *Don Juan* or the three used by Offenbach in his opera. Dumas says that the story was first told to him by Nodier; the papers of Paul Lacroix left to the Arsenal Library show that he too at least had a hand in drawing up Dumas's scenario for it;[1] but the writing is emphatically Dumas near his best. Originally published alone (1851), it is now usually included with the macabre tales of vampires and severed heads that Dumas issued in 1849–50 under the collective title *Les Mille et un Fantômes (The Thousand and One Phantoms),* stories in which the occult merges with the terror and horror of the Gothic novel. A different kind of tale of Germanic origin is *Othon l'Archer,* a version of the legend opera-lovers will recognize as the source of Wagner's *Lohengrin. Isaac Laquedem* (1853) is the first and only volume of a projected "epic" novel in twenty-five volumes based on the legend of the Wandering Jew. This book recounts the story of Jesus;

censorship forced abandonment of the rest of the series. *Le Père la Ruine* (1860), a somber story of Marne fishermen told with moving simplicity and sobriety, may well be Dumas's most sustained tragic work.

The list could go on but the point, we trust, is made. Among the many and varied works that compose Dumas's nonhistorical fiction five merit a slightly longer look. All of them may be loosely categorized as *romans de moeurs*, but each is something more as well.[2] The subject of *Georges* is racial conflict; *Les Frères corses* is an absorbing psychological study with supernatural overtones; *Conscience l'Innocent, Catherine Blum*, and *Le Meneur de loups*— along with parts of *Ange Pitou*—constitute Dumas's fictional tribute to the town and region of his birth.

I   Georges

Georges appeared in 1843, just the year before *Les Trois Mousquetaires*, and perhaps partly for that reason has tended to remain less known and less read than it deserves to be. Not ranking among Dumas's masterpieces, it is nonetheless a solid, well-written book. Of particular interest today because of its subject matter, it offers typical Dumasian appeal also in its exotic setting and adventurous story.

Georges Munier, the hero, is one of two sons of Pierre Munier, a wealthy mulatto planter of the Isle of France—an island east of Madagascar known today as Mauritius. Despite his wealth and personal qualities, Pierre Munier had decided he could best live vis-à-vis the white ruling class of the island by complete subservience: "his entire life was spent apologizing for his birth." His sons were sent to Europe to school in 1810, not to return for fourteen years. Though only twelve when he left, the sensitive Georges had already borne all the affronts he could from the whites—in particular young Henri de Malmédie—and determined that, unlike his father, he would devote his life to a "war to the death against prejudice." To that end he spent his years in Paris and London developing his mental, moral, and physical capacities to the maximum, especially his force of will and self-control. Following his formal education, Georges travelled extensively in Greece and the Near East and won the crosses of the Légion d'Honneur and of Charles III of Spain for his bravery in the battle of Trocadero. His brother had a different kind of life, going to sea and eventually becoming a slave trader: "Indeed, by a strange coincidence, chance brought together in one family the man who had spent his life bowed down under the prejudice of color, the man who made his fortune by exploiting it, and the man who was ready to risk his life to fight it."

After his return Georges falls in love with Sara de Malmédie, cousin and fiancée of his enemy Henri, and she is drawn to him. When Georges, who has thus far remained incognito, reveals his identity at the English governor's ball, Sara alone among the creoles there remains sympathetic. Georges determines to win her; he goes through the formality of asking for her hand, but is neither surprised nor dissuaded by her uncle's refusal. Georges is asked by Laïza, a slave he has freed, to serve as leader of an uprising of the slaves. When he learns that Henri de Malmédie, whom he has deliberately insulted, refuses to fight a duel with him, a mulatto, Georges agrees to Laïza's request but is tricked and imprisoned by the governor.

The uprising fails for lack of a leader and because the English forestall it by lighting the city and leaving barrels of liquor about to tempt the invading blacks. Georges escapes from prison and joins the few hundred blacks who are fighting the English, but the cause is lost. Recaptured and condemned to death by the English, in another *coup de théâtre* Georges escapes again, with Sara, to his brother's boat. A sea chase ensues and battle is engaged, but the English are defeated and the governor goes down with his ship.

It is difficult to read this novel without feeling that in it Dumas, like his hero, is fighting a prejudice. Because the prejudice is one that Dumas himself occasionally encountered, more than one commentator has identified Dumas with Georges. J.-H. Bornecque, for example,[3] sees Georges as an anticipation of Edmond Dantès both as superman and as the author's vicarious instrument of vengeance against a mediocre or rejecting society. One would be reluctant to go farther than this, if even this far, since Dumas's life is manifestly so different from that of his character. Unquestionably he experienced slights and insults—some of the worst being found in Mirecourt's pamphlet—but there is little evidence to suggest that he was deeply wounded by them, even less to suggest that he brooded over them. Certainly he never experienced the kind of ostracism and rejection of which Georges was a victim. In a cogent essay, "Dumas et les Noirs," ("Dumas and the Blacks"), Léon-François Hoffmann[4] reminds readers that, unlike Georges, Dumas was readily accepted in all circles in which he moved—indeed adulated in many—and that in the memoirs and in his letters he gives no hint of defensiveness or sensitivity about his lineage. Correspondingly, Hoffmann adds, he does not seem to find it a matter for special pride either; he does not even state in his memoirs that the grandmother whose name he bore was black. Though Dumas in all probability expressed his honest convictions about racial prejudice in *Georges*, it seems at the very least unlikely that the book was a deeply felt crusade or personal vindication.

Hoffmann points out another aspect of the book that emerges with careful reading: it is not a "black" novel in the usual sense of the word. The hero is a mulatto, and the prejudice he fights is quite clearly that directed against his mixed blood. Georges and his father both own black slaves[5] and Jacques, the slave trader, is depicted as breaking the law but by no means as a reprehensible person. Indeed, slavery as an institution does not seem to be seriously questioned, and Dumas seems more attracted by the paradoxical contrast of views within the Munier family than moved to support or denounce any of them. Further, except for Laïza and his brother the blacks in the book are shown as inferior beings. It is not by accident that Pierre Munier's intelligence and other fine qualities shine forth when he is in the company of blacks—as opposed to the whites who force him automatically into his self-deprecatory role—or that the slaves planning a revolt should look to Georges for the leadership they apparently could not find in their own numbers. If Dumas's life offers little support for theories that his novel is a calculated attack on antiblack prejudice in the nineteenth century, the novel suggests that he tended to share rather than to challenge his century's views.

In the light of the foregoing one may argue that for Dumas slavery or the status of the black man (or even the mulatto) as such was not at issue in this book. George's mixed blood, rather, appears exactly comparable to Antony's illegitimacy or Kean's profession: it is the pretext for a prejudice that keeps a superior man from participating in society. Georges joins the company of outcast Romantic heroes, exceptional individuals barred from their due by the laws, conventions, or prejudices of men less gifted than they. Dumas does not deny the reality of the injustice; he deplores it. But as was true in *Antony*, his approach is from the standpoint of the specific individual in the concrete situation rather than on the level of principle.

II Les Frères corses

The Corsican Brothers is a brief work, scarcely more than a long short story. It is cast in the form of the anecdotes in the *Impressions de voyage* and is narrated throughout in the first person by Dumas, who consequently plays a small role. The other characters were also real people, whom Dumas met on a visit to Corsica[6] and in Paris on his return.

The story is a simple one that falls naturally into two parts. In Corsica Dumas is lodged in the home of the de Franchi family, in the room of Louis de Franchi, one of his hostess's twin sons. The other son, Lucien, shows him around the house and village (Sullacaro), and tells how his parents had ended a vendetta of many years by simultaneously killing—in different places—the last two members of the enemy family. In the course of conversation Lucien describes the almost telepathic communication that exists between him and Louis, though Louis has chosen to settle in Paris and "be French" while Lucien has vowed to remain always Corsican. Reference is also made to Louis's lack of skill with a pistol in contrast to Lucien's expertise. During his visit Dumas witnesses the peaceful settlement of a vendetta between two families in which Lucien, almost annoyed with himself for doing it, serves as arbiter. When Dumas returns to Paris he takes with him a letter of introduction to Louis de Franchi.

Back in Paris Dumas establishes contact with Louis, for whom he soon finds himself serving as second in a duel with a young man named Château-Renaud.[7] Before the duel Louis writes a letter to his mother telling her he is dying of a brain fever, and informs Dumas that the ghost of his father had visited him during the night and told him he would die at 9:10 A.M. Mortally wounded in the duel, it is precisely at that time that Louis dies.

About five days later Lucien arrives in Paris, having seen his brother in a vision or dream the night before his death. He also says he knows the rest of what happened and has come, with his mother's blessing, to avenge Louis's death. Château-Renaud accepts Lucien's terms for a duel at the same place and with the same weapons. Lucien remains utterly calm, kills Château-Renaud as he predicted he would, then throws himself into Dumas's arms, weeping for the first time in his life.

The first thing that strikes the reader of this tale is the simplicity and economy of its telling, qualities not often held to be Dumas's forte. It lacks the controlled spareness of Mérimée's Corsican stories, but Dumas has found and maintained exactly the right tone for himself. Descriptions are vivid, characters and atmosphere are sketched with precision and force; there is scarcely a superfluous detail or word, and the action moves smoothly and relentlessly to its climax. Nothing is overstated, nothing distracts from unity or mood.

It is this straightforwardness and restraint that help Dumas to make the supernatural elements so convincing. They are, quite simply, there; and the reader accepts them with no need for explanation or justification. Unlike the spectacular display of Joseph Balsamo's powers, these visions—or ghostly visits, who is to say?—somehow do not strain the credulity or clash with the sober realism of their context. Similarly, the very simplicity of the characters lends them a moving nobility that enlarges their humanity as it deepens the meaning of the tale.

III   The Villers-Cotterêts Novels

"And, in point of fact, was it not in Villers-Cotterêts that I really and truly lived, since it was there that I waited for life?" So wrote Dumas in Chapter I of Catherine Blum. The affection he always felt for his native town, so apparent in even the most incidental allusions, overflowed in the 1850's in the series of novels Dumas based on recollections of his childhood and youth. The writing and publication of his memoirs occupied the first half of that decade and doubtless stimulated his memory, for the links between these novels and Mes Mémoires are many and close. By coincidence it was during the same period that Dumas wrote Ange Pitou and in that fact surely lies the explanation of its barely disguised transposition from his own life.

The earliest of the group, Conscience l'Innocent, is also the longest. Jean Manscourt received his nickname—the title of the book—because of his simplicity and absolute candor. After a quiet childhood in the village of Haramont, remote from the great events of the Napoleonic era, in 1813 Conscience—just eighteen—is called up for military service. His grandfather, who is dependent on him, tries unsuccessfully to buy a replacement. Knowing that a friend was discharged because of the loss of two fingers, Conscience chops off his right index finger. Accused of trying to avoid service, Conscience unhesitatingly admits his intent but persuades the authorities that he did not do it for himself. He escapes punishment and is taken on as a *soldat de train*. Eventually drawn into combat anyhow, he is blinded. His childhood sweetheart Mariette secures his release from the hospital in Laon and brings him home. Slowly his sight is regained. In 1815 when Napoleon passes through Villers-Cotterêts en route to Waterloo, Mariette and Conscience are in the throng waiting to greet him. The emperor speaks to them, gives Conscience a *croix de guerre* and Mariette an apronful of gold.

For about the first three-quarters of its length *Conscience l'Innocent* maintains a disarming simplicity and charm. Though idealized and sentimental, its depiction of peasant characters and life is sufficiently realistic and unaffected not to cloy. Conscience especially is well drawn, believable, and appealing despite his alarming perfection of character and fondness for talking to animals and flowers. Unfortunately, midway through the second volume the slight tale becomes unduly drawn out and repetitious and the ending is too contrived to satisfy.

Catherine Blum more successfully balances substance and length, at least partly, perhaps, because Dumas has concentrated all the action in a single day. A final chapter serves as epilogue to inform the reader of the longer-range consequences of the day's events.

Catherine returns to the home of her uncle Guillaume Watrin in Villers-Cotterêts after eighteen months in Paris learning millinery. During her absence she and her cousin Bernard Watrin realize that they love each other, but obstacles arise in their path. Bernard's mother opposes their marriage because Catherine is Protestant (her father was German); Louis Chollet, a Parisian, also seeks Catherine's hand; and a malevolent villager, Mathieu Gogolue, is trying to avenge an insult from Bernard. His plan for vengeance takes the form of a trick to deceive Bernard into thinking that Catherine is having clandestine meetings with Chollet. Mathieu's deception is eventually exposed, Mme Watrin is reconciled to the marriage, and all ends happily.

Like *Conscience l'Innocent*, *Catherine Blum* is a story whose chief merit is charm. It is again sentimental but its humor and brevity keep it from being maudlin or overly sweet. Perhaps its most surprising element is the cruelty shown by most of the characters toward the crippled Mathieu. Dumas apparently thought that Mathieu's viciousness was sufficient justification for the others' treatment of him and makes no attempt to excuse or conceal it. A modern reader might well find a major cause of Mathieu's meanness and vindictiveness in the attitudes of the others, and in Dumas's seeming lack of sympathy another example of the kind of acceptance of prevailing views that we observed in *Georges*.

Le Meneur de loups (The Wolf-Leader) joins Dumas's affection for his *petite patrie* to his predilection for tales of the supernatural. The story of a werewolf, it is a legend of the forest of Villers-Cotterêts told to him by old Mocquet, his father's *garde*. It has all the flavor of ghost stories told around a campfire, complete with the eerie reality of strange events in a familiar setting. Dumas precedes it with a lively account of a real wolf-hunt that prepares the way beautifully by familiarizing the reader with the setting and subtly suggesting the mysteries to be revealed. The story itself is a mingling of local legend and the universal tale of a pact with the devil: the covetous and ambitious young sabotmaker Thibault trades his soul for the fulfillment of his wishes, but reaps only unhappiness as each desire leads to another until the tragic dénouement.

These three novels cannot be ranked among Dumas's important works, but they deserve to be less neglected than they have been—especially *Catherine Blum* and *Le Meneur de loups*. Besides their intrinsic attractiveness they reveal a side of Dumas which he himself always took seriously, and they demonstrate his ability to work on an intimate scale at subdued volume. All three are filled with beautiful evocations of nature—especially the forest—and suffused with love for his native corner of France. To read them is to discover a different Dumas and to understand the familiar one in different ways, as he turns from the dazzling colors of history and adventure to the tranquil contemplation of a quieter world that is no less rich for him.

Why should I not love to speak of that immense bower of verdure, where every single object is fraught with memories of the past? I knew everyone and everything there; not only the people of the town, not only the stones of the houses, but even more the trees of the forest. . . . I will teach you the language of all those old friends of my youth, whether they be living or dead, and you will then understand with what gentle voices they breathe into my ear.[8]

CHAPTER 11

Dumas in Center Stage

I *The Tireless Traveler*

FOR nearly forty years Dumas's life was criss-crossed by journeys. In the 1830's he visited Switzerland, Italy, Germany (the Rhineland), and the South of France. After his marriage in 1840 he spent the better part of three years living in Florence and in 1846 undertook a three-month tour of Spain and North Africa. The next decade is framed by a two-year stay in Brussels (December, 1851, to November, 1853) interrupted by frequent visits to Paris, and his trip to Russia, which lasted from June, 1858, until March of the following year. In 1857 he had made a brief sojourn in England; in May, 1860, he was off again on the Schooner *Emma* for Italy—to join Garibaldi and to stay for almost four years. The summer of 1866 saw Dumas on the road once more, this time to Italy, Austria and Germany. Dumas's last visit to southern France, where he had gone for the sake of his health in the spring of 1870, was ended by the declaration of war. After that he travelled only back to the North. The last four and a half months of his life were spent quietly, with his daughter Marie at his side, in a house owned by his son at Puys on the Normandy coast.

Dumas's travels were undertaken for a variety of reasons. He went to Switzerland, he tells us, on his doctor's orders after a bout with cholera and overwork; it was also prudent on his part to absent himself from Paris after his involvement in the *journées de juin* (1832) made him somewhat suspect in politically conservative circles. He went to Germany with Gérard de Nerval at least in part as a distraction after his mother's death. He went to Spain to attend a royal wedding and to Algeria at the request of the minister of public instruction. He went to Russia—a nine-month journey on five days' notice—simply because he was invited to visit friends. His stay in Belgium was a self-imposed exile, ostensibly for political reasons, in reality because it also put him conveniently out of the reach of his creditors. But whatever the immediate reason, Dumas always travelled also because he loved to. His enthusiasm shows on every page of the *impressions de voyage* that record all his journeys except those to England and to Brussels.[1]

Not surprisingly, Dumas's travel impressions are not like those of contemporaries such as Gautier, Hugo, or George Sand, nor are they conventional travel books. They are Dumas himself seeing the world in his own special way. And never, surely, was there a writer more ready to see the world as a stage and all the people in it as actors. Travel for Dumas was like history: perceptible and express-ible in dramatic terms. He was not insensible to the natural beauty he observed, nor do descriptions of it lack in his books. Works of art and architecture too are given their due. But what most absorbed Dumas was the color and picturesqueness, the drama and the mystery of the lives that were lived in these settings. His travel books are filled with anecdotes and conversations, impressions of the people he travelled with, met, or was told about, and vivid evocations of historical events or local legends. In his novels he recreates people and events remote in time; in his travel books he captures the character and atmosphere of life remote in space or circumstances.

Such a tale as *Les Frères corses* with its intense drama, exotic setting, and picturesque mores could as readily as not have been included in a volume of *impressions de voyage*. Many like it are already there. The story of the French travelling salesman Alcide Jollivet who killed an Englishman in a hair-raising duel (*En Suisse*, Chapter XXIII–IV), for instance, is a comparably gripping narrative and study of character types. And though these characters are not native to the area in which the events take place, the setting still colors the story, which in turn becomes a subject of discussion among the local peasants and the basis for examination of their superstitions relative to Mount Pilatus.

In *Le Midi de la France (The South of France)* Dumas, contrary to his general tendency in *En Suisse,* uses principally humorous anecdotes to evoke the *caractère méridional,* this contrast alone revealing something of his perceptions. He recounts a hunt for *macreuses*—a bony, bad-tasting duck—on the Étang de Berre, for example, and he ends the book with the magnificent "shaggy dog story" of *La Chasse au chastre (Thrush Hunting)*. This tale starts as a simple illustration of the *Marseillais*'s passion for hunting and his persistence and total ineptness at it. As the luckless hunter pursues his elusive prey across the Riviera and into Italy, through encounters with friends, capture by bandits, and hairbreadth but slapstick escapes, the tale expands in every direction, a superb example of the imagination as well as the temperament Dumas is depicting.

De Paris à Cadix (Adventures in Spain) includes humorous, pathetic, and dramatic anecdotes among its vivid descriptions and animated accounts of bullfights, unbelievable coach rides, and the lavish festivities surrounding the marriage of the Infanta of Spain and the Duc de Montpensier. On their way to the Escorial Dumas and his companions do not encounter the bandits they were warned they might meet, but are forced to play at being bandits themselves—albeit paying ones—in order to procure the supper and lodging they want at the inn where they stop. In Seville they fall under the spell of a group of Spanish dancers in the theater and at a ball; in a subsequent visit to the home of Carmen, the youngest of the group, they learn the touching reality of her impoverished life away from the glitter and glamor of the stage. A visit to Seneca's house in Cordoba turns out to be a visit to a house of prostitution; the whole episode is recounted with a discreet formality that reflects the atmosphere of the evening and—Dumas says—the Spanish attitude toward the "oldest profession" and its practitioners. The paradoxical juxtaposition of frank sensuality and rigid propriety revealed in both these episodes has parallels in the many instances of equally paradoxical mixtures of banditry and the Spaniard's impeccable sense of honor. None is more impressive or entertaining than the story of a picnic and a hunt among the bandits of the Sierra Morena.

Nothing heightens Dumas's pleasure in visiting a place so much as knowing that on that spot something had happened. The something that happened then inevitably becomes a story to be told. The bridge in Montereau, Dumas's first stop on the way to Switzerland, inspires two chapters of dramatic historical anecdote that evoke the murder of John of Burgundy in 1419 and a bloody Napoleonic battle nearly four centuries later. In Lyon, on the way to Provence, the sites associated with Cinq-Mars and Thou call forth tales of their lives as well as reminiscences of Vigny's novel in which they figured. One of the most celebrated anecdotes from the same

journey is the chilling account of the murder of Maréchal Brune in
room No. 3 of the Hôtel du Palais-Royal in Avignon, the room
Dumas—a godson of Brune—asked to occupy when he was there.
Dumas's first glimpse of the Escorial elicits an anecdote (of
somewhat dubious authenticity) about its building; and the entrance
gate to the Alhambra is not crossed without calling to mind
Ferdinand's victory and the expulsion of the Moors from Granada.

But Dumas's anecdotes not only bring to life the people and
customs he observes, the history and lore he absorbs. They even
help him on occasion to define landscape or atmosphere. When he
visits Les Baux de Provence the overwhelming sensation he
experiences at this bleak and rugged site is one of sadness. How
much more vividly the sensation and the setting are conveyed to the
reader when Dumas then describes the funeral of a beggar child that
he witnessed in the church on that lonely, windswept promontory.
Or how better could the barren emptiness of La Crau in 1834 be
evoked than by the hilarious account of a stop at the invisible town
of Bouc, midway between Arles and Martigues? The town existed,
as the plan of streets and buildings and the decree establishing
it—signed by Napoleon in 1811—could prove. But it could not be
seen in any direction on that endless rocky plain for the excellent
reason that, except for the inn at which Dumas and Jadin stopped
and two empty houses, it had never been built.

Everything interests Dumas and everything is fodder for his
memory or his imagination. Though he ordinarily made notes at
night while travelling and wrote his printer's copy later from the
notes, his travel books all retain the spontaneity and casual
organization of fresh impressions jotted down on the spot as they
came to him. The narrative of the journey may be—and often is—
interrupted by digressions as Dumas is reminded by something of
some other place, event, or person. En route to Russia in 1858, for
instance, his crossing of the Rhine calls to mind—and pen—the
Rhenish tour he made with Gérard de Nerval twenty years before.
In the same fashion, a stop at Waterloo on his way to meet Nerval
then had revived memories of Napoleon's passage through Villers-
Cotterêts in 1815, and he let that story divert him from the account
of the travels he was engaged in.[2] Nor does he hesitate to
intersperse large chunks of background or historical information he
wants his readers to have. The Russian journey is again a case in
point with its extensive history of the Romanoff family; and even his

slim volume on the French Midi devotes two full chapters to a
history of Marseille from its founding to 1789—admittedly borrowed
directly from a history of Provence by Louis Méry.

But such interpolations—like the translations from Pushkin that
he includes in the *Voyage en Russie* or the legends he records at
length in *Les Bords du Rhin*—do not damage the works. They too
are part and parcel of Dumas's travel experiences and it seems only
natural that they should be shared along with everything else that
he chooses to report or comment on. Rather than distractions they
are like pauses en route for a second look or like forays into inviting
side roads to see where they lead. For the form of Dumas's travel
books is simply the form of the journeys themselves. Quite regularly
he begins with an explanation of the circumstances leading to his
departure and a more or less lengthy account of the lives and
personalities of his travelling companions; he then proceeds from
one place to the next chronologically, if not always in a straight line,
and ends with a terse "In four days I was back in Paris," or words to
that effect. The tone is intimate, varied, and lively, that of a relaxed
after-dinner chat with friends or a personal letter from a gifted
correspondent who is not pressed to finish his letter quickly. Dumas
has had a good time on his trip, he implies; now it is his reader's turn
to be entertained and to be led, in Maurois's happy image, less from
city to city than from tale to tale.[3]

The *Impressions de voyage* are filled also with memorable
portraits of the people Dumas met in the course of his travels, the
friends he journeyed with or went to see, the celebrities whose
paths he crossed. His depictions of Gérard de Nerval, of the ageing
Chateaubriand in Lucerne, of Queen Hortense—step-daughter of
Napoleon—in her "castle" of Arenenberg are justly famous. But the
fullest and most compelling portrait to emerge from these pages is
that of Dumas himself—a giant of a man with a giant curiosity, ever
ready for new experiences and new friends, for new adventures and
new horizons. We see his pride over decorations bestowed on him
by the kings of Belgium and Spain and his equally great delight over
a glass of wine offered him by the little dancer in Seville. We share
his pleasure at dinners with princes or in modest country inns, his
discomfort on the roads of Spain, his awe before the Alps, his hearty
laughter on a hundred occasions. We experience his emotion at
meeting—in Russia—the people whose story he had written in a
novel two decades before,[4] his exhilaration at finding his name

known in the most unlikely places from Finland to North Africa, his
satisfaction at showing ladies in Switzerland or an innkeeper in
Spain how a proper omelet should be cooked or a salad dressed.
There are few better ways to come to know Dumas than through
these magical pages, the still-living record of some of his happiest
days.[5]

I confess that the best and sweetest memories of my life are those of such
jaunts made in Switzerland, Germany and France, in Corsica and Italy,
Sicily and Calabria, whether jointly with a friend or alone with my thoughts.
Things when you actually see 'them often seem only commonplace, but the
moment you look back at them in memory they take on a tinge of poetry
that you would never have believed memory could adorn them with. . . .[6]

II *Backward Glances*

Dumas's memoirs were written in Paris, Brussels, and again Paris
between 1851 and 1855. They were published serially in *La Presse*
until Dumas returned to Paris and founded his journal *Le
Mousquetaire;* in it he printed the *nouvelle série* that first appeared
in book form under the somewhat misleading title *Souvenirs de 1830
à 1842.*[7] Some three thousand pages in all, ten volumes in the
standard edition, to record the recollections of thirty-two years!

In characteristically grandiose fashion Dumas viewed *Mes
Mémoires* not as his alone but as "the literary archives of the first half
of the nineteenth century," the record of "the painting, the poetry,
the literature and politics of the first fifty years of the century."[8]
Allowing for hyperbole—and the fact that he stopped well short of
the midpoint of the century—we can still acknowledge validity in
his claims, for Dumas has given in this work a panorama of his times
that is rich in both sweep and detail. It is a marvellous gallery of
portraits of Dumas's famous contemporaries—Charles Nodier at the
Arsenal, the young Musset reading his *Contes d'Espagne et d'Italie,*
Victor Hugo, Vigny, and other artists, writers, actors, and
politicians. It recounts fondly and admiringly the exploits of General
Dumas and his misfortunes along with the lives and deeds of
obscure but dear friends. It is a vivid, animated account of great
events and small, of life in Villers-Cotterêts and revolutions in Paris,
of theatrical premières, lawsuits, duels, and military missions. It is
larded with discussions of the works of others and it is stuffed with
quotations, not only from others but on occasion from Dumas

himself.[9] It contains accounts of events that he did not witness as well as events that he did; but where he relies on newspapers and other published sources for his facts (and sometimes a bit more),[10] in his inimitable retelling he usually contrives to make those accounts his own.

Despite his claims, however, Dumas's memoirs are not entirely a work of history and obviously not a systematic one. Loose ends and repetitions are frequent and inaccuracies abound. *Mes Mémoires* were written, after all, from memory and—like almost everything else Dumas wrote—too hurriedly. As a consequence they need correction[11] at many points where memory failed or haste betrayed. But like the novels, *Mes Mémoires* remain true in their broad lines, their depiction of personalities, their evocation of milieu and atmosphere, their re-creation of a period. They are true also in the colorful, revealing, and exact details of daily life and manners that cram their pages. In all this they continue to be a useful document for the student of the nineteenth century. But their greatest value and greatest interest do not lie precisely there. Dumas may indeed have aspired to chronicle his century, but he titled his work "*My* Memoirs," and it is the portrait Dumas gives of himself—both in what he says and the way he says it—that constitutes the real treasure of these bulky volumes, as of the *Impressions de voyage.*

The Dumas we already know from the novels and plays is there, more concrete and more complete, more flamboyant and more alive than ever. His pretentiousness and conceit at times appear enormous, yet he can be honestly modest as well as honestly proud of his achievements. His judgments of his contemporaries may sometimes lack in perspicacity, but his image of himself at least as often surprises by its realistic shrewdness. His recollections of himself as a country lad in Picardy and as a struggling young provincial in Paris, spun out in loving detail, are alternately amusing and touching. He was not unaware of his strengths as a writer—we have noted his comments on the structure of *Henri III et sa cour*— but he was also aware of his limitations and he speaks of both with equal frankness. His endless delight in his own exploits is matched by his zest in talking about them.

This marathon display of himself and his opinions is balanced by sincerity, a disarming candor, and one other quality that perhaps is the most important of all: a total absence of pettiness. Dumas is never less than fair, more often generous, most often lavish, here as in every facet of his life. This alone redeems much in the *Mémoires;* charm and vitality do the rest.

Three thousand pages to recount only the first three decades of a life that lasted for seven and whose fullest years lay beyond the memoirs' stopping point. The story of that life is partially completed in the few miscellaneous books of *souvenirs,*[12] in the travel impressions, and in such works as *Les Garibaldiens* (*On Board the* Emma), which relates the events of Dumas's first few months in Italy with Garibaldi. But in *Mes Mémoires* alone Dumas has written—it has become almost commonplace to remark—his greatest adventure story of them all. And he has carved a place beside Edmond Dantès and d'Artagnan for its hero.

CHAPTER 12

Conclusion

"**D**UMAS *père* was what Gounod called Mozart, a summit of art." So wrote George Bernard Shaw in 1893;[1] and he continued, "you get nothing above Dumas on his own mountain: he is the summit, and if you pass him you come down on the other side instead of getting higher."

A definition of "Dumas's mountain" has been one of the goals of this study. If we have succeeded in suggesting what it is, we have also indicated, we trust, what it is not. A clear awareness of what any writer did not attempt to do is prerequisite to fair appraisal of what he did; such awareness is nowhere more needed than in the case of Dumas *père*—awareness not only of what he did not try to do but of what he was not.

There is little point or profit in faulting Dumas because he was not a highly cultivated man of letters, a meticulous stylist and craftsman of refined and sensitive tastes, a scholar or a thinker. These were simply not his attributes. He was not a subtle Stendhal writing for the "Happy Few," though he clearly shared Stendhal's cult of energy; nor was he a visionary Balzac, though his gifts as an observer were in their way not inferior to those of the author of the *Comédie Humaine*. Temperamentally, intellectually, and artistically Dumas was far removed from Lamartine and Hugo, Vigny and Musset, though he knew and appreciated them all. What Dumas was we have seen: a largely self-educated country boy of boundless imagination whose youthful enthusiasms persisted undiminished throughout his life; a man of action endowed with inexhaustible energy and curiosity; a born storyteller with a matchless flair for drama; a writer whose craft was more instinctive than learned.

The year of his death Dumas was described in the Larousse *Grand Dictionnaire universel du XIXe siècle* as "a novelist and the most prolific and popular playwright in France."[2] The popularity enjoyed by his plays a hundred years ago waned with the nineteenth century—a recent limited revival of interest notwithstanding—but Dumas's place in the history of the French theater seems now more secure than ever. He created two important genres, the prose historical drama and the *drame moderne*. He dominated the popular theater with some of the most successful melodramas, dramas, and comedies that reached the boards. His creations and his successes left their mark both in the directions they pointed and the imitations they inspired.

But while his plays have been relegated to history, the best of Dumas's fiction remains a living part of France's literary patrimony. Less dated by their form than the plays, the novels are also richer in universal qualities. In them Dumas not only exploits his dramatic sense but indulges his gifts for storytelling as well as dialogue, for making the remote seem real and immediate, for leisurely and expansive development of character. He explores a wider range of human emotions and finds more responsive chords to touch in his readers' hearts. In the novels too we meet the characters whose names and deeds have become household words wherever the books have penetrated. Dumas to his delight found himself known from Finland to North Africa, from England to Astrakhan; today even fewer corners of the world would be so isolated as never to have heard of d'Artagnan and the Musketeers, of the Count of Monte-Cristo or the Man in the Iron Mask.

The volumes of memoirs and personal reminiscence and, especially, the travel books share many of the strengths of Dumas's fiction but their fate has been nearer that of his plays—without the compensating acknowledgment of historical importance. Their neglect is regrettable since it is justified neither by their value nor by their interest. *Mes Mémoires,* whatever their inaccuracies of detail, remain an absorbing and illuminating document; the *Impressions de voyage* are no less amusing or true[3] for lacking the descriptive precision of the travel books of a Théophile Gautier or the style of a Victor Hugo. In contrast to these works, Dumas's "historical compilations" are appropriately left today to those who wish to evaluate his knowledge of history and pinpoint his sources.

Unlike many of his Romantic contemporaries, unlike some of his own heroes, Dumas did not reject the values of the bourgeois society in which he lived. He was able to deplore its vices and wrongs, but he also held fast to and glorified its dreams and aspirations. His successful heroes were supermen who not only broke the bonds that limit ordinary mortals but who positively attained the goals and embodied the ideals of those same ordinary men. Georges Munier, Edmond Dantès, d'Artagnan, or Chicot may possibly be viewed as sublimations of Dumas's frustrations or as his vicarious vengeance on society. They unquestionably represent a surrogate for the mass of Dumas's readers who through them can still escape the dullness of daily life and vicariously realize their dreams. For if Dumas embraced the outlook and values of his age he went beyond them as well. The motives of his characters and, consequently, the themes of his works are the great human drives of love, loyalty, and friendship; hate, jealousy, and vengeance; the struggle for power, the acceptance of duty, the giving and the affirming of self. Timeless and universal in themselves, so are their interest and appeal.

Dumas never wrote for an elite but always for the widest possible audience. This was less a conscious decision on his part than a natural concomitant of his life and character. He was by nature, as he himself observed, a popularizer. He was also a showman, and what he lacked in depth he made up in breadth and brilliance. Though we may not look to him for profundity, that is not to say there is nothing to learn from him. At the same time, however, though we may learn from Dumas, his primary aim is never to teach. Above all else he seeks to provide his readers with pleasure—a pleasure as old as listening to stories. He belongs to the illustrious line of tellers of tales that began with the ancient bards and inventors of fables, that includes medieval troubadours who sang of love and high adventure, the narrator of the exotic wonders of the *Arabian Nights,* and all those others whose goal has been to delight and divert. Dumas is a supreme entertainer, able to free us from our world without severing its ties, refreshing us as he uncovers amazing vistas we had not seen or shines an enchanted light on those we had thought familiar. Such gifts as his are rare; he uses them with an art to be admired as well as enjoyed.

Notes and References

Chapter One

1. Alexandre Dumas, *Mes Mémoires* (Paris: Michel Lévy, 1863), 10 vols., ch. XXVIII. Further references to this work will use the abbreviation *MM* followed by chapter number. Pierre Josserand observes the Lévy chapter numbering in his five-volume edition of *Mes Mémoires* (Paris: Gallimard, 1954–68); his notes were most helpful in the preparation of Chapters 1, 2, and 11 of the present study.
2. *Ibid.*, XXXIX.
3. Later co-author of the libretto for Adolphe Adam's popular opera *Le Postillon de Longjumeau* and director of the Opéra-Comique, de Leuven was the son of Count Adolphe-Louis Ribbing de Leuven, one of the three noblemen involved in the assassination of King Gustave III of Sweden.
4. Hippolyte Parigot, *Alexandre Dumas père* (Paris: Hachette, 1902), p. 15. While Dumas does not specifically say so in his memoirs, it is a very likely assumption.
5. Written in 1822, this text is printed for the first time in volume I of Dumas's *Théâtre complet*, ed. Fernande Bassan (Paris: Lettres Modernes-Minard, 1974).
6. *MM*, LXXIX.
7. *Ibid.*, LXXX.
8. In 1833 Harriet Smithson married the composer Hector Berlioz. After their marriage Dumas helped organize a special performance of *Antony* and the fourth act of *Hamlet* for their benefit as they were in severe financial difficulties. Berlioz remarks in his memoirs (Paris: Garnier-Flammarion, 1969), II, 293: "Alexandre Dumas . . . all his life has been wonderfully gracious to me." In 1836 Edmund Kean became the subject of a play by Dumas.
9. Marie Mennessier-Nodier, *Charles Nodier, Épisodes et souvenirs de sa vie* (Paris: Didier, 1867), pp. 291–97. Cf. *MM*, CXXI.

Chapter Two

1. *MM*, CXVII–CXIX.
2. *The Spirit of the Holy League.* Dumas does not identify the book in his memoirs but specified the title in his 1833 essay "Comment je devins auteur dramatique," later published as the general introduction to his *Théâtre complet*.
3. Following Dumas's published *Théâtre complet*, the date of the première has always been given as February 11. In *Alexandre Dumas père*

147

et la Comédie-Française (Paris: Lettres Modernes-Minard, 1972), p. 27, Fernande Bassan and Sylvie Chevalley correct this 125-year-old error.

4. *MM*, CXIX.

5. Parigot, p. 30.

6. *MM*, CXVIII.

7. For a severe and explicit critique of Dumas's style in *Henri III* and several other plays, see A. Brun, *Deux Proses de Théâtre*, Pub. des Annales de la Faculté des Lettres, Aix-en-Provence, Nouvelle série n° 6 (Gap: Ophrys, 1954), pp. 23–33. Among other faults, Brun points out that Dumas's sixteenth century nobles speak the popular language of 1830.

8. Alfred de Vigny vigorously defended Dumas's right to distort history this way. Juste Olivier quotes Vigny as saying, "By combining the stories and transforming the sieur de Monsoreau into the duc de Guise he has elevated the play, made it poetic. A play in which historical fact and the Lady of Monsoreau's amorous adventures were scrupulously observed would not have been at all poetic. It would only have been an obscure and bourgeois *'aventure de ménage'* " (*Paris en 1830: Journal*, ed. André Delattre and Marc Denkinger [Paris: Mercure de France, 1951], pp. 103–4).

9. *MM*, CXXXI.

10. *Ibid.*, CXXXIII.

11. *Ibid.* The memory of this evening and that "melodious echo" of poetry may well have contributed to Dumas's determination to leave his play in verse despite Harel's urging that he redo it in prose.

12. *Ibid.*, CXXXVII.

13. *Antony* had been brewing for some time in his mind, as revealed by his correspondence with Mélanie Waldor. The actual composition, completed in June, 1830, dated from the day six weeks earlier when he suddenly had the idea for the ending (see *Ibid.*, CXXXVI). Vigny commented on this characteristic of Dumas's method of composition in an article about the play, "Album: A propos d'*Antony*" (*Revue des Deux-Mondes*, II [mai 1831], p. 326).

14. *MM*, CLXXIV. According to Dumas, Harel locked him in a room in the apartment of the actress Mlle George with all necessary books and writing materials, releasing him only when the last act had been written and the entire play read aloud to Harel and a group of his actors.

15. *MM*, CLXXIV and CLXXXV.

16. *Ibid.*, CC.

17. It is perhaps not entirely coincidental that in 1831 Dumas legally acknowledged as his the daughter born that year to him and Bell Krelsamer, as well as the son (Alexandre *fils*) born to him and Catherine Labay in 1824.

18. Cf. Jules Janin, *Le Journal des Débats*, 5 mai 1831: "M. Dumas has seen fit to put the preface of his drama in the fourth act and to explain . . . his literary and dramatic system in the middle of the action."

19. The difficulties that faced dramatists who chose to write contemporary plays were not limited to questionable reactions from the public, as Dumas was to be reminded in 1834 when a revival of *Antony* at the Comédie-Française was cancelled because of the "obscenity" of the play, and again in 1838 when the revival of *Angèle* in the same house was closed after a few performances. "Like *Antony, Angèle* presented a modern situation whose audacity could not be tolerated in a state theater" (Sylvie Chevalley, "Dumas et la Comédie-Française," *Europe*, no. 48 [février-mars 1970], pp. 103–4.)

20. André Maurois, *Les Trois Dumas* (Paris: Le Livre de Poche, 1957), p. 106.

21. Albert Thibaudet, *Histoire de la littérature française de 1789 à nos jours* (Paris: Librairie Stock, 1936), p. 192. We quote from the translation by Charles Lam Markmann, *French Literature from 1795 to our era* (New York: Funk & Wagnalls, 1967), p. 170.

22. So says Hippolyte Parigot in *Le Drame d'Alexandre Dumas* (Paris: Calmann-Lévy, 1899), p. 176. Dumas, writing from memory twenty years after the event, reports "some two or three hundred" performances between 1832 and 1834 *(MM*, CCXXXVI).

23. *MM*, CCXXXIV.

24. In reality her sisters-in-law, the wives of the two brothers of Marguerite's husband, King Louis X. There is apparently no basis in fact for the legends of Marguerite's orgies, though she was accused of adultery and imprisoned in the Château Gaillard in Normandy. There she was suffocated by order of the king, who was anxious to remarry. Somewhat later, after the death of her husband (Philippe V), Jeanne returned to live in the tower. She led a notoriously dissipated life there and more than once her lover-of-a-night was found in the Seine the next day. In all probability this is the origin of the reputation later attributed to Marguerite and the basis for the legends of the tower.

25. As Maurois and others have pointed out, if Dumas were really concerned here with historical events, this date would make Marguerite a mother at the age of three.

26. André Le Breton, *Le Théâtre romantique* (Paris: Boivin, n.d.), p. 31.

27. Cf. Parigot, *Alexandre Dumas père*, p. 101.

28. And most of Dumas's biographers since. See, for example, Henri Clouard, *Alexandre Dumas* (Paris: Albin Michel, 1955), p. 175; and Parigot, *Alexandre Dumas père*, pp. 94–5.

29. Maurois, pp. 171–2.

30. F. W. Reed, *A Bibliography of Alexandre Dumas père* (London: J. A. Neuhuys, 1933), p. 137.

31. Parigot, *Alexandre Dumas père*, p. 108. To the contrary, Sylvie Chevalley ("Dumas et la Comédie-Française," pp. 103–4), finds this play *"aimable"* and worthy of success equal to that of *Mademoiselle de Belle-Isle;*

and G: B. Shaw gave a glowing review to an 1897 English production (see *Our Theatres in the Nineties* [London: Constable, 1932], III, pp. 158–62).

32. A. Craig Bell, *Alexandre Dumas: A Biography and Study* (London: Cassell, 1950), p. 133.

33. *Ibid.*, p. 134.

Chapter Three

1. Though his name appeared on no playbills in 1835 or 1840, in both years Dumas collaborated with others on new plays produced then.

2. In 1847, for his Théâtre Historique, Dumas produced two important adaptations from foreign plays: *Intrigue et Amour*, a translation of Schiller's *Kabale und Liebe*; and his version of *Hamlet*, based on a translation by Paul Meurice who was listed as co-author. The few changes and omissions Dumas made in Schiller's play actually tightened and clarified the action; the extent to which he and Meurice altered Shakespeare may be suggested by the fact that in their version Hamlet does not die in the end. Rejected by the Comédie-Française in 1848, this *Hamlet* entered the repertory there for a number of years after Dumas's death.

3. Parigot, *Le Drame d'Alexandre Dumas*, p. 182.

4. For a penetrating study of this ambiguity in relation to the structure of the plays and their political implications, see Annie Ubersfeld, "Désordre et Génie," *Europe*, no. 48 (février-mars 1970), pp. 107–19. I am indebted to this excellent article also for ideas developed in my discussion of *Kean;* notably that of Kean's "three dilemmas."

5. In his 1953 adaptation of this play Jean-Paul Sartre changes Kean's role in this episode to Othello—historically one of Kean's greatest roles, dramatically an inspired change.

6. Chevalley, "Dumas et la Comédie-Française," p. 101. Dumas wrote or collaborated on at least ninety plays that were produced during his lifetime. The standard *Théâtre complet* (Michel Lévy, 1863–74) contains sixty-six plays. The new edition undertaken by Minard promises 123 plays, sketches, and fragments, many previously unpublished or even generally unknown.

7. Parigot, *Le Drame d'Alexandre Dumas*, p. 419.

8. *Ibid.*, p. 420.

9. Brun, *Deux Proses de Théâtre*, pp. 23, 31–2.

10. Many of Dumas's contemporaries, however, held one of his greatest strengths as a dramatist to be his skill in depicting complex and living characters. Vigny, for example, in his article on *Antony*, devotes more than three pages to a detailed and glowing appreciation of the psychological and dramatic validity of Antony and Adèle. George Sand, dedicating her drama *Molière* (1851) to Dumas, praises him for having proved that "the interior man can be sufficiently revealed within the limited proportions of a play" and that powerful dramatic action need not preclude analysis of character.

Chapter Four

1. For this discussion I have used Dumas's introduction as printed in the second edition of the novel (Paris: Alexandre Cadot, 1848), pp. 3–30; all quoted passages are from this source. Internal evidence suggests that though published with *La Comtesse de Salisbury* the preface may well have been written for *Isabel de Bavière*.

2. Clouard, p. 253; Gilbert Sigaux, preface to the *Pléiade* edition of *Les Trois Mousquetaires* and *Vingt Ans après* (Paris: Gallimard, 1966), p. xii.

Chapter Five

1. The story of the queen's diamonds is recounted in the memoirs of several persons, among them those of the duc de La Rochefoucauld, author of the celebrated *Maximes*. The reader who wishes to pursue in detail the relationship between history and invention in the d'Artagnan cycle is referred to the editions of the novels prepared by Charles Samaran (*Classiques Garnier*) and Gilbert Sigaux (*Editions Rencontre* and *Pléiade*). I am indebted to both these scholars for much of the factual information incorporated into my discussion of Dumas and his sources.

2. Gilbert Sigaux, preface to volume 1 of *Les Trois Mousquetaires* (Lausanne: Editions Rencontre, 1962), p. 15.

3. Charles Samaran, introduction to *Les Trois Mousquetaires* (Paris: Garnier, 1956), p. xix.

4. *Ibid.*, pp. 123, 168 (notes).

5. Sigaux, preface to *Les Trois Mousquetaires* (Editions Rencontre), p. 9.

6. The American film director Samuel Fuller has observed: "D'Artagnan entering Paris on a worn-out horse is exactly the same as a cowboy arriving in a little western town. . . . Dumas is the father of the American western, but no one has ever said so." (Quoted by Claude Baignières in *Le Figaro*, 1 November 1974, p. 12.) The allusion, obviously, is to the opening scene of *Les Trois Mousquetaires*, and hence should read *Meung*, not *Paris*.

7. This episode gives another excellent illustration of Dumas's simplification of history for dramatic effect. Historically there were two flights of the court, the first in September 1648 to Reuil, the second in January 1649 to Saint-Germain. A third one was attempted in 1651, in circumstances similar to those described by Dumas, but was unsuccessful.

8. Robert Louis Stevenson, "A Gossip on a Novel of Dumas's," in *Memories and Portraits* (New York: Charles Scribner's Sons, 1912), pp. 212–28. The quotation is from p. 216.

9. *Ibid.*, pp. 220–21.

10. Bell, p. 199.

11. Stevenson, p. 225.

Chapter Six

1. Sigaux, in his preface to the Rencontre edition of *Les Quarante-Cinq* (p. 11), states that Dumas had planned a concluding novel for the series that was to center on the assassination of the duc de Guise in 1588.

2. The name is more correctly "de Sauves"; we follow Dumas's spelling, as with La Mole and Coconnas (historically La Molle and Coconat).

3. Readers of Stendhal will recognize in La Mole the much admired ancestor of Mathilde de la Mole in *Le Rouge et le Noir*, and in Marguerite the mistress who bought her lover's severed head from the executioner. Though there is no proof for the historicity of this anecdote, it is not held to be either impossible or implausible. Cf. Sigaux, preface to volume 2 of *La Reine Margot* (Lausanne: Editions Rencontre, 1967), p. 13.

4. Antoine Blondin, introduction to *La Dame de Monsoreau* (Paris: Le Livre de Poche, 1967), I, 6–7.

Chapter Seven

1. With characteristic inadvertence, Dumas introduces him as Georges de Charny in Chapter V, later changing his name to Olivier. In *Ange Pitou* a younger brother named Georges dies protecting the royal family the night of October 5–6, 1789. Similarly, Dumas makes Andrée some six years younger than Marie-Antoinette in this novel, a change in conflict with her age in *Joseph Balsamo*.

2. Despite the duplication of title, Morand, the chevalier de Maison-Rouge of this novel, has no connection with Philippe de Taverney, chevalier de Maison-Rouge, who figures in *Joseph Balsamo* and its sequels.

3. Gilbert Sigaux, preface to volume 1 of *La Comtesse de Charny* (Lausanne: Editions Rencontre, 1965), p. 10.

4. *Ibid.*, pp. 10–11.

Chapter Eight

1. Sigaux, preface to *La Comtesse de Charny* (Editions Rencontre), p. 8.

2. In his *Causeries* ([Paris: Michel Lévy, 1860], I, 5), Dumas observes: "Lamartine is a dreamer; Hugo is a thinker; as for me, I am a popularizer."

3. Clouard, pp. 350–72; Sigaux, prefaces to *Les Trois Mousquetaires* and *Vingt Ans après* (Pléiade), pp. xii–xxi, and *Vingt Ans après* (Rencontre), II, 7–22. Parigot (*Le Drame d'Alexandre Dumas*) and Maurois (*Les Trois Dumas*) also provide well-reasoned and fair examinations of the question. The Garnier editions of *Les Trois Mousquetaires* and *Le Comte de Monte-Cristo* reprint the existing fragments of Maquet's outlines and notes for those two novels. My discussion is based on all of these sources; I lay no claim to original research or interpretation.

4. Mirecourt published libelous brochures about many writers and prominent figures during the 1840's and 50's—George Sand and Alfred de Musset among others—but none created a greater scandal or public outcry than his attack on Dumas.

5. Clouard, pp. 365, 356.
6. Sigaux, prefaces to *Les Trois Mousquetaires* and *Vingt Ans après* (Pléiade) and volume 2 of *Vingt Ans après* (Rencontre).
7. Sigaux, introduction to volume 2 of *Vingt Ans après* (Rencontre), p. 22.

Chapter Nine

1. The date is probable, not verified. Cf. C. Samaran, introduction to *Les Trois Mousquetaires* (Paris: Garnier, 1956), p. xii (note 1). J.-H. Bornecque in his edition of *Le Comte de Monte-Cristo* (Paris: Garnier, 1962) places the incident in 1843 (see pp. iv and lxxii).
2. *Causeries* (Paris: Michel Lévy, 1860), vol. I, pp. 263 ff.
3. *Le Diamant et la Vengeance,* by Jacques Peuchet, was published in 1838 as part of a six-volume work called *Mémoires tirés des archives de la police de Paris.* In his *causerie* Dumas refers to it as *La Police dévoilée.* He printed Peuchet's tale with *Le Comte de Monte-Cristo* in the second printing of the edition published *"Au Bureau de l'Écho des Feuilletons"* in 1846.
4. The abbé Faria was not merely Dumas's equivalent in the novel of the Italian prelate imprisoned with François Picaud; a real abbé Faria existed and almost certainly provided Dumas with some characteristics as well as a name. Cf. Sigaux, preface to *Le Comte de Monte-Cristo* (Editions Rencontre), pp. 15–16; Clouard, p. 301; Bornecque, preface to *Le Comte de Monte-Cristo* (Garnier).
5. Bornecque, pp. xlii–li.
6. *Ibid.,* p. xliii.
7. Sigaux, preface to *Monte-Cristo* (Editions Rencontre), p. 15.
8. Completed in 1847, the "château" was a house as extravagant and fantastic in its appointments as anything in the *Arabian Nights;* its architect was one of Dumas's stage designers at the Théâtre-Historique. Maurois and Clouard, along with many others, describe the house and grounds as well as the celebrated party that opened Dumas's residence there. Dumas himself reminisces about Monte-Cristo and its menagerie of exotic pets in *Histoire de mes Bêtes.* Barely a year after he occupied it Dumas was forced to move out and eventually sold it for less than a tenth of its cost in order to pay off debts. The building still stands, externally at least in woefully dilapidated condition.

Chapter Ten

1. Clouard, p. 244.
2. A further point in common is that all are among the works Dumas wrote without collaborators. The only one whose authorship is disputed at all is *Georges.* Mirecourt asserted that it had been written by Félicien Mallefille, but Dumas insisted that it was his own and there is little reason to doubt his word.

3. Bornecque, preface to *Monte-Cristo* (Garnier), pp. lxii ff.

4. Léon-François Hoffmann, introduction to his edition of *Georges* (Paris: Gallimard, Collection Folio, 1974).

5. Dumas's father toó had a black servant, though obviously not a slave; cf. *Mes Mémoires*, Chapter XVI, and Chapter 2 of *Le Meneur de loups*. A black servant accompanied Dumas on his trip to Spain (Cf. *De Paris à Cadix*, Chapter 2 and *passim*).

6. Clouard (p. 242) places Dumas's trip to Corsica in 1842, during his travels with Prince Napoleon: In the story Dumas specifies the date as early March, 1841.

7. Dumas gives the same name to one of the young dandies in the circle of Albert de Morcerf in *Le Comte de Monte-Cristo*.

8. "Prologue" (Chapter I) to *Catherine Blum*.

Chapter Eleven

1. Dumas does, however, devote the first ten chapters of *Excursions sur les Bords du Rhin (Travels Along the Rhine)* to an account of his visits to a number of Belgian cities and his dinner with King Leopold in Malines. All this occurred in September, 1838, while Dumas was on his way to meet Nerval in Frankfurt.

2. He was to retell the story, in altered form, in *Conscience l'Innocent* and in his memoirs, both written in the early 1850's.

3. André Maurois, preface to Dumas's *Voyage en Russie*, ed. Jacques Suffel (Paris: Hermann, 1960), pp. 11–12.

4. In 1840 Dumas had published a short novel entitled *Le Maître d'Armes (The Fencing Master)* that was based on a true story told to him by a friend who had been in Russia. In it a young Russian cavalry officer, condemned to hard labor in Siberia after the Decembrist conspiracy in 1825, was followed into exile—in the dead of winter—by his mistress, a Parisian milliner who had been living in Moscow. This couple, the Count and Countess Annenkov, were introduced to Dumas in Nizhniy-Novgorod; the meeting was one of the high points of his trip to Russia.

5. Dumas's four travel books on Italy possess the same qualities as those we have discussed in this chapter; they differ chiefly in growing from many visits and extended acquaintance with that country and its people rather than from a single trip. Their titles are *Une Année à Florence (A Year in Florence)*, *La Villa Palmieri*, *Le Corricolo* and *Le Speronare*. (The Villa Palmieri was the house in which Boccaccio wrote the *Decameron*. The *Speronare* was the boat that took Dumas to see Sicily, while *Corricolo* was the name given to a carriage in Naples.)

6. *Midi de la France*, Chapter 21.

7. The title is inaccurate since the memoirs were never finished. The period covered extends only to 1834, with no more than incidental reference to later events.

8. *MM*, CCLXIII and CCVII.

9. One example of the latter will suffice. In 1833 Dumas wrote an essay on his start as a dramatist, "Comment je devins auteur dramatique," for the *Revue des Deux-Mondes*. From 1836 on it served as general introduction to editions of his collected plays. It is reprinted in *Mes Mémoires* with only insignificant changes.

10. Pierre Josserand, preface to his edition of *Mes Mémoires*, I, 14.

11. A task admirably performed by Josserand in his notes.

12. The *Causeries*, *Histoire de mes Bêtes* (1868), *Souvenirs dramatiques* (1868).

Chapter Twelve

1. George Bernard Shaw, *Our Theatres in the Nineties* (London: Constable, 1932), III, 189.

2. *Grand Dictionnaire universel du XIXe siècle*, vol. 6, (Paris: Larousse, 1870), p. 1373.

3. Clouard, p. 213, quotes Miguel de Unamuno, who stated that he found Dumas's and Gautier's books about Spain more essentially true than any more scientific or scholarly works he knew.

Selected Bibliography

PRIMARY SOURCES

The standard edition of Dumas is the *Oeuvres complètes* in 301 volumes published by Michel Lévy, later Calmann-Lévy, beginning in 1851. Unfortunately this edition is considerably less than definitive or really complete; it is unannotated and many volumes are exceedingly difficult to find. Most of Dumas has been reprinted, however, and at least the best-known works are readily obtainable in French or English. We have made no attempt to cull the mass of popular editions and translations, but list below the most authoritative and useful edited versions that have appeared in recent years.

Oeuvres d'Alexandre Dumas père. Ed. Gilbert Sigaux. 38 vols. Lausanne: Editions Rencontre, 1962–67. This series contains the following fifteen novels, all accompanied by excellent introductions:

Les Trois Mousquetaires	*Les Deux Diane*
Vingt Ans après	*La Reine Margot*
Le Vicomte de Bragelonne	*La Dame de Monsoreau*
Le Comte de Monte-Cristo	*Les Quarante-Cinq*
Joseph Balsamo	*Le Chevalier de Maison-Rouge*
Le Collier de la Reine	*Les Blancs et les Bleus*
Ange Pitou	*Les Compagnons de Jéhu*
La Comtesse de Charny	

Mes Mémoires. Ed. Pierre Josserand. 5 vols. Paris: Gallimard, collection "Mémoires du passé pour servir au temps présent," 1954–68.
Théâtre complet. Ed. Fernande Bassan. Many volumes projected. Paris: Lettres Modernes-Minard, Collection "Bibliothèque introuvable," 1974– .
Antony. Ed. Joseph Varro. Paris: Larousse, "Nouveaux Classiques Larousse," 1970.
Le Comte de Monte-Cristo. Ed. J.-H. Bornecque. 2 vols. Paris: Garnier, 1962.
Georges. Ed. Léon-François Hoffmann. Paris: Gallimard, Collection "Folio," 1974.

Kean. Adaptation by Jean-Paul Sartre (Dumas's text appended). Paris: Gallimard, 1954.
Les Trois Mousquetaires. Ed. Charles Samaran. Paris: Garnier, 1956. Rpt. 1966.
Vingt Ans après. Ed. Charles Samaran. Paris: Garnier, 1962.
Les Trois Mousquetaires. Vingt Ans après. Ed. Gilbert Sigaux. Paris: Gallimard, Bibliothèque de la Pléiade, 1962. Rpt. 1966.
Voyage en Russie. Ed. Jacques Suffel, preface by André Maurois. Paris: Hermann, 1960.

A NOTE ABOUT TRANSLATIONS

Substantially all of Dumas's fiction has been translated into English, some of it many times over during the past hundred years, and all but the most obscure novels can be located with relative ease. Translations of the plays, on the other hand, where they exist at all, are extremely difficult to find. An excellent abridged translation of Dumas's memoirs has been published under the title *The Road to Monte-Cristo* by Jules Eckert Goodman (New York: Scribner, 1956). A. C. Bell has also translated portions of the memoirs as well as a variety of other nonfictional works by Dumas. Abridged translations from the travel writings done by Alma Elizabeth Murch can likewise be recommended. *On Board the* Emma (London: Ernest Benn, 1929), R. S. Garnett's translation of *Les Garibaldiens*, is more complete than standard French versions as it incorporates material Dumas intended to include in reprintings but did not. Garnett has also translated Garibaldi's memoirs as edited and revised by Dumas (New York: D. Appleton, 1931).

SECONDARY SOURCES

Books and articles about Dumas are even more numerous than his own writings. Again we list only the most important or interesting among fairly recent works, plus a few still valuable earlier studies. Other books and articles consulted in the preparation of this volume are indicated in the footnotes.

BASSAN, FERNANDE, and SYLVIE CHEVALLEY. *Alexandre Dumas père et la Comédie-Française*. Bibliothèque de Littérature et d'Histoire, no. 15. Paris: Lettres Modernes-Minard, 1972. Detailed and informative study of all matters relative to the production of Dumas's plays by this company.
BELL, A. CRAIG. *Alexandre Dumas: A Biography and Study*. London: Cassell, 1950. Not completely satisfactory as either biography or study, it nevertheless contains valuable bibliographies and much useful information, especially about Dumas's journalistic activities.

BLAZE DE BURY, [ANGE] HENRI. *Mes Études et mes souvenirs: Alexandre Dumas, sa vie, son temps, son oeuvre.* Paris: Calmann-Lévy, 1885. Sympathetic recollections of Dumas and interesting comments on his writings, especially the plays. One of the best nineteenth century studies.

BOUVIER-AJAM, MAURICE. *Alexandre Dumas ou Cent Ans après.* Paris: Les Éditeurs Français Réunis, 1972. Lively, provocative study, especially interesting on Dumas's political ideas and methods of work, though some conclusions are debatable.

CLOUARD, HENRI. *Alexandre Dumas.* Paris: Albin Michel, 1954. Unquestionably the best general study of the life and works of Dumas *père*, unfortunately without bibliography or index and never translated into English.

Europe, no. 48. Février-Mars 1970. A special issue of the magazine devoted to articles about Dumas on the occasion of the centenary of his death. All are interesting though of variable merit.

GORMAN, HERBERT. *The Incredible Marquis: Alexandre Dumas.* New York: Farrar and Rinehart, 1929. A quite reliable and very entertaining popular biography.

MAUROIS, ANDRÉ. *Alexandre Dumas: A Great Life in Brief.* Trans. Jack Palmer White. New York: Alfred A. Knopf, 1966. Good, readable introduction to Dumas's life, quite obviously adapted from parts of the next entry.

————. *Les Trois Dumas.* Paris: Hachette, 1957. Rpt. Le Livre de Poche, 1957. *The Titans, a Three-Generation Biography of the Dumas.* Trans. Gerard Hopkins. New York: Harper and Row, 1957. The authoritative biography of Dumas *père*, his father, and his son. Excellent bibliography and index in Hachette and Harper editions, omitted in Livre de Poche.

MIRECOURT, EUGÈNE DE. *Fabrique de Romans, Maison Alexandre Dumas et compagnie.* Paris: Tous les Marchands de Nouveautés, 1845. The famous attack on Dumas.

PARIGOT, HIPPOLYTE. *Alexandre Dumas père.* Paris: Hachette, "Les Grands Écrivains français," 1902. Still one of the very best studies of Dumas's work: balanced, perceptive, and fair.

————. *Le Drame d'Alexandre Dumas: Étude dramatique, sociale et littéraire.* Paris: Calmann-Lévy, 1899. Parigot's *thèse*, the classic and irreplaceable study of Dumas's plays.

REED, FRANK WILDE. *A Bibliography of Alexandre Dumas père.* London: J. A. Neuhuys, 1933. An indispensable key for entry into the bibliographical maze of Dumas's published works and a few unpublished ones. Ten typewritten supplements are owned by the British Museum.

SIMON, GUSTAVE. *Histoire d'une collaboration: Alexandre Dumas et Auguste Maquet.* Paris: Crès, 1919. One of the first attempts to study the question of Dumas's collaborations from documents, Simon's pro-Maquet conclusions have been effectively qualified by later scholars.

Index

161